Plants

and

Animals

The Editors of Larousse

PETER BEDRICK BOOKS
NTC/Contemporary Publishing Group

This volume forms part of the Young People's Encyclopaedia. It was produced under the editorial direction of Claude Naudin, Catherine Boulègue, and Nathalie Bailleux. Text contributors: Roger Dajoz, Guilhem Lesaffre, Eric Mathivet, and François Moutou, assisted by Olivier Cornu, Sylvie Daumal, and Marie-Claude Germain.

Graphic design and art direction by Anne Boyer, assisted by Emmanuel Chaspoul
Layout by Laure Massin
Proofreading, revision by Annick Valade, assisted by Isabelle Dupré and Françoise Moulard
Picture editing by Anne-Marie Moyse-Jaubert
Picture research by Marie-Annick Réveillon
Production by Annie Botrel
Technical coordination by Pierre Taillemite
Page makeup by Palimpseste
Cover by Gérard Fritsch, assisted by Véronique Laporte

Original title:
Les Plantes et Animaux

English translation by
Donald Gecewicz

First published in the United States in 2000 by Peter Bedrick Books
A division of NTC/Contemporary Publishing Group, Inc.
4255 West Touhy Avenue
Lincolnwood (Chicago), Illinois
60712-1975 U.S.A.
Copyright © 1995 by Larousse-Bordas
Translation copyright © 2000 by NTC/Contemporary Publishing Group, Inc.
Printed in France
International Standard Book Number:
0-87226-623-0

00 01 02 03   8 7 6 5 4 3 2 1

Discover the Peter Bedric

Plants and Animals

In this volume, the diversity of life on our planet is revealed page by page from the most simple to the most highly evolved species, ranging from algae to orchids, from sponges to insects, from fishes to monkeys.

how to use this book

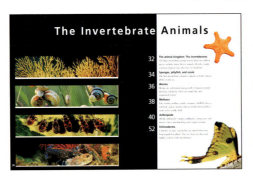

The Invertebrate Animals

This volume is divided into three sections. Every section is introduced by a contents list that sets out the various chapters and gives a short summary of each.

Special picture-spreads are included between the chapters to reproduce exceptional images, including a chameleon's snack and the desert meerkats.

The closing pages contain remarkable facts and biographies of famous biologists and naturalists.

Finally, an index helps you to find quickly the page containing the information you are looking for.

LIVIN

oung People's Encyclopedia

chapter title
Each chapter unfolds over either one or two spreads.

introductory text
This summarizes the broad outline of the subject to be described in the chapter.

panoramic photograph
This illustrates one of the topics of the chapter.

margins
These contain information on additional subjects.

In the natural world, there are plants that never produce flowers: the algae, lichens, mosses, ferns, and conifers. Each of these plants has its own method of reproduction.

The nonflowering plants

a giant brown seaweed: kelp (*Macrocystis pyrifera*)

- **cryptogam:** nonflowering plant with reproductive organs that are usually hidden or inconspicuous.
- **gamete:** male or female reproductive cell that can join with a gamete of the opposite sex to form a new living organism.
- **gymnosperm:** nonflowering plant with seeds that are naked; that is, not protected within a fruit.
- **plankton:** mass of minute animals and plants that live floating in water.
- **rhizome:** an underground stem, usually horizontal, that produces roots growing downwards and leaves or stems bearing leaves.
- **sporangium:** in ferns, a type of pouch or case containing spores.
- **spore:** very small seed that some vegetative species, such as fungi, mosses, and ferns, use for their reproduction.
- **thallus:** plant body of an alga or fungus in which roots, stem, and leaves are not differentiated.

A brown alga
(*Fucus vesiculosus*).

The nonflowering plants were the first plants to appear on Earth. Some of them, the **cryptogams** (from the Greek *kryptos*, "hidden," and *gamos*, "marriage"), have either inconspicuous or sometimes hidden reproductive organs. These include the algae, lichens, mosses, and ferns. Others, the **gymnosperms** (from the Greek *gymnos*, "naked," and *sperma*, "seed"), produce seeds not protected by a casing: these are the conifers.

This red seaweed (*Phyllophora*) lives in salt water at great depths.

Green, brown, and red algae

The algae are the most ancient of all the plants. Most algae live in water. They have a very simple structure in which roots, stem, and leaves are merged in a single visible unit, called the **thallus**. There are algae of every size. Some are microscopic, like the diatoms that float in the oceans and form part of plant **plankton**. There are other huge species such as *Laminaria*, brown seaweeds that can reach nearly 4 m (13 ft) in length, or sargasso weeds, dozens of meters in length. Algae also have different shapes: some are made up of a simple strand (continuous or with offshoots), others have a flattened form or are round with more or less indented edges.

There are three divisions of algae distinguished by the color of their pigment: green algae, brown algae, and red algae. Green algae (such as the sea lettuce or the *Spirogyra*) have only one green pigment, chlorophyll. Brown algae (such as *Fucus*) also have brown and yellow pigments, while red algae contain red and blue pigments. Algae use these pigments to feed.

To grow, they also need water and light. Brown algae are found only in salt water, while green and red algae also grow in fresh water. There are some algae that have managed to evolve out of water, such as the *Chlorococcus* algae, which live in damp places on tree bark or on old walls.

Algae reproduction

Algae reproduce by diverse and often very complicated methods. *Fucus*, a brown algae found on rocks, is a typical example. *Fucus* can be male or female, or both at the same time. At certain periods, swellings appear on the edges of the thallus. These enclose the reproductive organs that produce reproductive cells (or **gametes**), which are released into the water. Fertilization, the fusion of a male gamete with a female gamete, gives rise to a single cell, the egg, which grows into a new plant.

Lichens

In partnership with fungi, some microscopic single-celled algae form unique plants called lichens. The alga uses its chlorophyll to make the substances that feed the fungus. In return, the fungus serves as a water reservoir for the plant and supplies it with minerals. Lichens are plants that live only on land, growing on the ground or on tree trunks or stones.

Many lichens reproduce by fragmentation. For example, if a small piece of lichen containing a fragment of alga and fungus breaks off and becomes attached in a new position to a rock or tree trunk, it will give birth to a new lichen.

Lichens are usually grey, green, or yellow and take various shapes. Some, such as those of the *Cladonia* genus, look like small erect bushes. Lichens are very robust and can survive even on bare rock. They grow slowly but live for a very long time (some are probably more than 4,000 years old). They are found in all regions of the world, except in hot deserts, and are especially prevalent in cold regions such as the Arctic.

Spirogyra
A floating green alga, *Spirogyra* resembles a thread 1 to 2 cm (0.5 in) long and is made up of a row of completely identical cells. When two threads meet, as seen here with a microscope, the cells fuse. This is how the alga reproduces.

Part of these lichens (*Cladonia coccifera*) stands erect above the ground.

Diatoms
These microscopic algae, which are the basic element of plant plankton, are unicellular (made up of a single cell). Each cell is formed by a siliceous shell known as a frustule. As this microscope image of diatoms shows, the frustules vary in shape.

---

mini-dictionary
The difficult words, marked in bold in the text, are defined here.

heading
Each subsection expands on a basic aspect of the subject.

caption
Photographs and diagrams are always captioned and are in some cases accompanied by longer scientific or technical explanations.

C o n t

e n t s

The Plants

The plant kingdom

○ bacteria: general name given to microorganisms, made up of a single cell, that live in decomposed material or as parasites of humans, animals, and plants.

○ cell: the smallest constituent element of a living organism.

○ chlorophyll: the green pigment in the cells of most plants, which absorbs light and releases energy, and which enables plants to absorb carbon dioxide from the air and to give off oxygen.

○ microorganism: microscopic animal or plant organism.

○ ovule: female cell used for reproduction. In a flower, a small organ contained in the ovary of the pistil that changes into a seed after fertilization—that is, after combination with a pollen grain.

○ photosynthesis: process by which plants use chlorophyll to produce their nutrients. They absorb carbon dioxide from the air and water from the soil to make sugars and give off oxygen.

○ protists: a group of living things made up of a single cell with a distinct nucleus.

○ spermatozoid: male cell used for reproduction in many plant species.

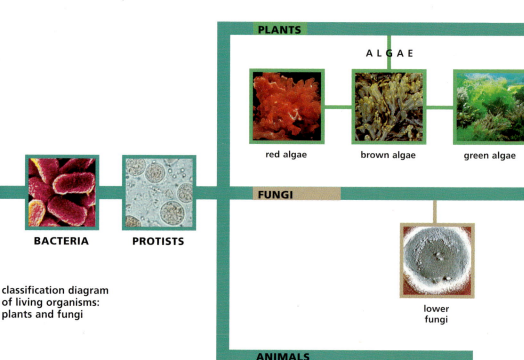

BACTERIA

PROTISTS

PLANTS

ALGAE

red algae

brown algae

green algae

FUNGI

lower fungi

ANIMALS

classification diagram of living organisms: plants and fungi

The first living organisms appeared in the oceans 3.5 billion years ago. They were primitive **bacteria**, formed of a single cell. Over billions of years, as the Earth's atmosphere underwent changes, these transformed and diversified. Some types of bacteria evolved that contained **chlorophyll**. The chemistry of these plant-bacteria led to the formation of an oxygen-rich atmosphere favorable for the development of other life forms.

Classification of living organisms
Living organisms have three properties. They are all made up of cells. They can all reproduce by creating descendants identical to themselves. They are all born, grow, and die. Apart from **microorganisms** (bacteria and **protists**), living organisms divide into three groups, or kingdoms, which can be defined according to the method by which they feed.

Plants (belonging to the plant kingdom) are distinguished by having chlorophyll and by their capacity to use the energy in sunlight to make their own nutrients from water and minerals in the soil and carbon dioxide in the air. Animals (comprising the animal kingdom) cannot use the sun's energy to make food. To survive and grow, they must eat other living organisms, either plants or animals. Fungi have no chlorophyll and, like animals, must find their nutrients in a form ready to eat. Fungi have unique characteristics, and so are classified as an entirely separate kingdom.

At present, some 100,000 fungi species, more than 300,000 species of plants, and 1.2 million animal species are known to exist. In the different kingdoms, species are classified and grouped by genus, family, order, class, and division. As the names of plants and animals vary from one country to another,

giant brown seaweed (*Macrocystis pyrifera*)

lichens

MOSSES

FERNS

CONIFERS

FLOWERING PLANTS

higher fungi

Photosynthesis

Tree roots draw water and minerals from the soil, which are carried along its vessels to the leaves as crude sap. There, by the action of chlorophyll, sunlight, and carbon dioxide, this raw sap is transformed into organic material (elaborated sap), which is distributed throughout the tree by other vessels. During this process, known as photosynthesis, the tree releases oxygen.

biologists have given each an international name derived from Latin. This name has two parts. The first indicates the genus and always starts with a capital letter, and the second gives the species. Thus, the wolf, *Canis lupus*, belongs to the genus *Canis* and to the species *lupus*.

The life of plants

Like animals, plants are born, grow, reproduce, and die. Unlike animals, plants have no nervous system, and therefore cannot make rapid movements. Although all plants have chlorophyll, their size and shape varies. Some, such as algae, are formed of a single element, but most are made up of roots, stalks, and leaves. Plants reproduce sexually by using male (**spermatozoids**) and female (**ovules**) sex cells. These cells are contained in organs that in algae, mosses, and ferns are small and concealed but that are clearly

visible in conifers and flowering plants in the form of cones or flowers. Plants also reproduce by forming new shoots or by separating into several pieces. This is known as asexual reproduction.

Using chlorophyll and the sun's energy, plants can make the organic material that they need for growth. This chemical reaction, known as **photosynthesis**, is of crucial importance, because besides extracting carbon dioxide from the air, plants also give off oxygen during the process. Over the course of time, plants have enriched the Earth's atmosphere with oxygen and created the conditions favorable for life on the planet. □

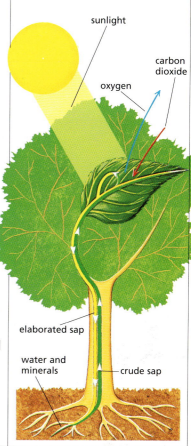

sunlight

carbon dioxide

oxygen

elaborated sap

water and minerals

crude sap

The

- **carpophore:** visible part of a fungus, usually made up of a stalk and cap and commonly known as a mushroom.
- **chlorophyll:** the green pigment in the cells of most plants, which absorbs light, releases energy, and enables plants to absorb carbon dioxide from the air and to give off oxygen.
- **mycelium:** hidden part of a fungus, made up of a network of underground threads, usually white.
- **mycorrhiza(s):** association of a lower fungus with the roots of a plant, which is beneficial for both parties.
- **mycosis:** skin disease caused by microscopic fungi.
- **parasite:** organism that lives on or in another organism from which it feeds.
- **pore:** very small opening at the end of a fungal tube.
- **spore:** very small seed that some vegetative species, such as fungi, mosses, and ferns use for their reproduction.
- **toxic:** poisonous, containing a substance dangerous to organisms.

Fungi form a numerous and diverse group of organisms distinct from both animals and plants. By feeding on dead plant matter, many fungi play an important role in the balance of nature.

fungi

Fungi constitute a group apart. Unlike plants, they do not contain **chlorophyll**. They feed on living or dead organisms, just as animals do. They have no roots, stalk, leaves, or flowers and reproduce in a unique fashion.

Lower and higher fungi

There are two types of fungi: the higher fungi such as chanterelles, and the lower fungi, which are tiny, even microscopic, such as molds and yeasts. The field mushroom is a typical higher fungus. It has a stalk surmounted by a cap. Beneath this cap are the gills, which are pink or blackish and radiate out like the spokes of a wheel. The stalk and the cap make up the **carpophore**, which is the visible part of the mushroom. In the soil, the fungus also extends a network of thin, fragile filaments. This is the **mycelium**, which acts like a root by extracting water and

nutrients from soil and plant debris.

Lower fungi have no carpophore but are made up solely of a mycelium. The most familiar are molds, which grow on food, and yeasts used in the making of beer and bread.

Fungi reproduction

The reproduction of the field mushroom is typical of higher fungi. Its carpophore (the stalk and cap) is in fact a sort of fruit; the gills of the cap produce millions of microscopic cells or **spores**, a type of small seed. These spores break away from the cap, fall to the ground, germinate, and produce a new mycelium. This grows gradually, and if it becomes joined to another mycelium, it forms a new carpophore—a new fungus. Fungus mycelia can live and grow for a very long time and can become huge. The lower fungi, which do not produce carpophores,

higher fungi: chanterelles (*Cantharellus cibarius*)

the fly agaric (*Amanita muscaria*), a toxic mushroom

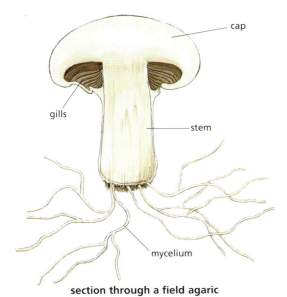

section through a field agaric

bear their spores directly on the mycelium.

Varied species

Fungi show a variety of forms. Some, including the boletus fungi, lack gills under their cap, while their surface, like a sponge, is made up of minuscule tubes. At the ends of these tubes are small holes or **pores**. In these pores, the spores essential for reproduction are formed. Morels have a very special shape: a conical cap pitted with small cavities. Truffles resemble small black potatoes and grow underground. Although some fungi such as morels and truffles are delicious to eat, others such as the fly agaric are poisonous and **toxic**, or even fatal like the death cap, for example.

An important role

Many fungi play a beneficial role in nature. To grow, they absorb nutrients from leaves and dead wood piled up on the ground. They thus help to decompose and break up plant matter that otherwise would rapidly choke forests. Other fungi (boletus, amanita,

and russula) form stains or **mycorrhizas**, non-harmful partnerships on the roots of trees such as pines, oaks, and chestnuts. Mycorrhizas cause the trees to absorb the substances they need for growth more readily, and the fungus takes advantage, in return, of shelter and nutrients. However, some fungi are harmful **parasites** that take their nutrients from living plants or animals. Examples are the rusts and smuts, lower fungi that can wipe out entire fields of wheat or maize. Other lower fungi parasitize humans by causing the sicknesses known as **mycoses**. ☐

Fairy rings

A fungus may have a network of underground threads with several stalks. These stalks sometimes appear in meadows, in regular circles known as fairy rings. This one is formed by stems of agarics (*Cortinarius alboviolaceus*).

Penicilliums

Microscopic fungi of the genus *Penicillium* grow on damp substances by forming molds, as above on a peach. Some species produce an antibiotic, penicillin, while other species are used in cheese making. A third group of penicilliums are toxic.

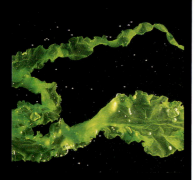

In the natural world, there are plants that never produce flowers: the algae, lichens, mosses, ferns, and conifers. Each of these plants has its own method of reproduction.

The nonflowering plan

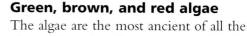

- **cryptogam:** nonflowering plant with reproductive organs that are usually hidden or inconspicuous.
- **gamete:** male or female reproductive cell that can join with a gamete of the opposite sex to form a new living organism.
- **gymnosperm:** nonflowering plant with seeds that are naked; that is, not protected within a fruit.
- **plankton:** mass of minute animals and plants that live floating in water.
- **rhizome:** an underground stem, usually horizontal, that produces roots growing downwards and leaves or stems bearing leaves.
- **sporangium:** in ferns, a type of pouch or case containing spores.
- **spore:** very small seed that some vegetative species, such as fungi, mosses, and ferns, use for their reproduction.
- **thallus:** plant body of an alga or fungus in which roots, stem, and leaves are not differentiated.

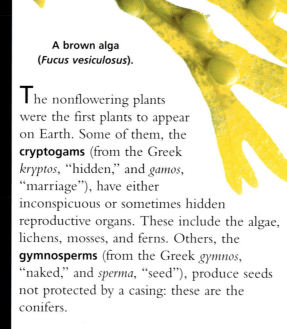

A brown alga
(*Fucus vesiculosus*).

The nonflowering plants were the first plants to appear on Earth. Some of them, the **cryptogams** (from the Greek *kryptos*, "hidden," and *gamos*, "marriage"), have either inconspicuous or sometimes hidden reproductive organs. These include the algae, lichens, mosses, and ferns. Others, the **gymnosperms** (from the Greek *gymnos*, "naked," and *sperma*, "seed"), produce seeds not protected by a casing: these are the conifers.

This red seaweed (*Phyllophora*) lives in salt water at great depths.

Green, brown, and red algae

The algae are the most ancient of all the plants. Most algae live in water. They have a very simple structure in which roots, stem, and leaves are merged in a single visible unit, called the **thallus**. There are algae of every size. Some are microscopic, like the diatoms that float in the oceans and form part of plant **plankton**. There are other huge species such as *Laminaria*, brown seaweeds that can reach nearly 4 m (13 ft) in length, or sargasso weeds, dozens of meters in length. Algae also have different shapes: some are made up of a simple strand (continuous or with offshoots), others have a flattened form or are round with more or less indented edges.

There are three divisions of algae distinguished by the color of their pigment: green algae, brown algae, and red algae. Green algae (such as the sea lettuce and the *Spirogyra*) have only one green pigment, chlorophyll. Brown algae (such as *Fucus*) also have brown and yellow pigments, while red algae contain red and blue pigments. Algae use these pigments to feed.

To grow, they also need water and light. Brown algae are found only in salt water, while green and red algae also grow in fresh water. There are some algae that have managed to evolve out of water, such as the *Chlorococcus* algae, which live in damp places on tree bark or on old walls.

Algae reproduction

Algae reproduce by diverse and often very complicated methods. *Fucus*, a brown algae found on rocks, is a typical example. *Fucus*

a giant brown seaweed: kelp (*Macrocystis pyrifera*)

can be male or female, or both at the same time. At certain periods, swellings appear on the edges of the thallus. These enclose the reproductive organs that produce reproductive cells (or **gametes**), which are released into the water. Fertilization, the fusion of a male gamete with a female gamete, gives rise to a single cell, the egg, which grows into a new plant.

Lichens

In partnership with fungi, some microscopic single-celled algae form unique plants called lichens. The alga uses its chlorophyll to make the substances that feed the fungus. In return, the fungus serves as a water reservoir for the plant and supplies it with minerals. Lichens are plants that live only on land, growing on the ground or on tree trunks or stones.

Many lichens reproduce by fragmentation. For example, if a small piece of lichen containing a fragment of alga and fungus breaks off and becomes attached in a new position to a rock or tree trunk, it will give birth to a new lichen.

Lichens are usually grey, green, or yellow and take various shapes. Some, such as those of the *Cladonia* genus, look like small erect bushes. Lichens are very robust and can survive even on bare rock. They grow slowly but live for a very long time (some are probably more than 4,000 years old). They are found in all regions of the world, except in hot deserts, and are especially prevalent in cold regions such as the Arctic. ☐

Spirogyra

A floating green alga, *Spirogyra* resembles a thread 1 to 2 cm (0.5 in) long and is made up of a row of completely identical cells. When two threads meet, as seen here with a microscope, the cells fuse. This is how the alga reproduces.

Part of these lichens (*Cladonia coccifera*) stands erect above the ground.

Diatoms

These microscopic algae, which are the basic element of plant plankton, are unicellular (made up of a single cell). Each cell is formed by a siliceous shell known as a frustule. As this microscope image of diatoms shows, the frustules vary in shape.

leaves of a moss (*Polytrichum*)

Mosses and ferns

Capsules of cord moss

At the tops of the stems of this moss (*Funaria hygrometrica*), magnified about 20 times, are small sacs, or capsules, containing spores. These capsules are green and turned toward the sun. When they mature they turn brown. They then open and the spores are scattered over the moist ground. When the spores germinate they produce new mosses.

Like the algae, mosses and ferns have no flowers. Their reproductive organs are not very conspicuous, which is why these plants are classified with the algae and lichens among the **cryptogams**. However, unlike algae, mosses and ferns have true stems covered with leaves.

Mosses and liverworts
Mosses are tiny plants that grow slowly. They have stalks and leaves but do not have true roots. These plants include the *Musci* or true mosses (for example, cord moss and polytrichum) and the sphagnums, or peat

mosses, which live in water. Liverworts (*Hepaticae*) have no stalks or leaves. Mosses and liverworts are mainly found in damp places, for they need water to grow and reproduce.

Moss reproduction
Cord moss (*Funaria hygrometrica*) is a true moss that grows in forests. It is made up of bright green leafed stems a few centimeters in height. Its reproduction is typical of mosses. In spring, barely visible male and female reproductive organs develop at the top of its stems. These organs contain reproductive cells, the **gametes**. The male gametes hold numerous spermatozoons, the female gametes a single oosphere (a type of ovule). The spermatozoons swim in the thin film of moisture that covers the moss (which is why this plant must grow in damp places) in search of the oosphere (which does not move). Fertilization occurs, producing an egg. The egg produces a fine stem tipped by a swelling, called the capsule. In this capsule the cells multiply to form numerous spores, which are like small seeds. When the capsule opens, the spores fall to the ground, germinate, and produce other mosses.

Different types of ferns
Ferns are very ancient plants. Their first ancestors, the rhynia, lived 400 million years ago, when giant tree ferns formed forests. Today there are more than 10,000 fern species, living mainly in wet areas: in forests (bracken and polypodium), in meadows

a tree fern (*Cyathea arborea*)

clusters of sporangia under a wall fern
(*Polypodium vulgare*)

germinate. Each spore then produces a **thallus**, a thin green blade on which male and female reproductive organs appear. Fertilization, or fusion of the gametes, produces an egg that becomes a new fern. ☐

An epiphytic fern

Some fern species (above, staghorn fern, *Platycerium*) grow on the trunks of trees. These are epiphytes, plants that feed on minerals found between the tree trunk and their own roots.

A fossil fern

Some 200 million years ago, a great part of the Earth was covered by hot, humid forests. Giant ferns grew to heights of 25 m (over 80 ft). The decomposition of these masses of ferns formed many coal deposits. In rocks dating from this, the Carboniferous period, fossil ferns such as this (*Pecopteris*) have been found.

(horsetail), and growing in cracks in rocks or walls (maidenhair).

Ferns are made up of roots, stems, and leaves. At the beginning of their development, the leaves, or fronds, are rolled up in a shape resembling a shepherd's crook. Then, little by little they unfurl. The stem, or **rhizome**, which bears the leaves, grows underground and has roots. The rhizome and roots are crossed by microscopic tubes, the vessels that allow sap to circulate around the whole plant. Ferns were the first plants to develop such a circulatory system. The size of ferns varies with the climate. In tropical regions, some species grow as large as trees and are known as tree ferns. In temperate zones, ferns are usually a lot smaller.

Fern reproduction

Under the leaves appear yellowish-orange organs, which look like small bags. These are **sporangia**, containing a great number of small seeds known as **spores**. When these spores are released and fall to the ground, they

a young fern leaf
(*Polystichum filix-mas*),
rolled up

forest of spruce (*Picea abies*) in France

Conifers and related plants

From pollen to pine cone

Like all conifers, this maritime pine (*Pinus pinaster*) bears cone-shaped fruits. The male cones supply the pollen grains, and the female cones hold the ovules. When an ovule is fertilized by pollen, the female cone expands (above, in the center of the photograph). It then gradually changes into a pine cone.

The conifers (the name means cone bearer) have cone-shaped reproductive organs. There are male cones and female cones. The seeds in the female cones are not protected by a casing. For this reason, conifers are called **gymnosperms**, or plants bearing naked seeds. Conifer leaves are usually shaped like needles, and most species do not shed them in winter. Most conifers are evergreen trees. Under their bark, they have ducts that secrete resin.

The conifers

Conifers withstand cold very well. They grow in the mountains and in cool regions, where they form the main part of the boreal forests, as well as in areas bordering the sea where the climate is milder. The best-known conifers are the pines (such as the Scotch pine, maritime pine and parasol pine) and the firs (like the silver fir, which forms large forests in the mountains of Europe). The conifer group also includes other trees, for instance cypresses, junipers, arborvitaes, spruces (including the common spruces sold as Christmas trees), cedars (cedar of Lebanon, for example), larches (such as the common larch), and sequoias (for example, the California redwood). The red-berried

common yew and the araucaria (including monkey-puzzle trees) are also conifers. The shapes of the conifers vary considerably. Most conifers, and in particular the pines, are used in timber industries where their wood is used for making paper, house construction, and carpentry, since these types of trees grow very quickly. Conifers include the oldest and largest trees in the world. In North America there are bristlecone pines (*Pinus aristata*) that are more than 4,000 years old and giant sequoias, goliaths of the plant world, which grow to a height of 100 m (over 320 ft).

Conifer reproduction

In conifers, the reproductive organs are grouped in their cones. An example is the Scotch pine, a conifer that bears small male cones (or male flowers), and female cones. When ripe, the male cones release great amounts of microscopic yellow grains, the pollen. Transported by the wind, the pollen grain comes into contact with a female cone, germinates, and forms a tube containing two male **gametes**. Fertilization with a female gamete produces an egg that slowly transforms into a seed. During this transformation, the female cone grows larger and changes into the familiar pine cone. When the scales of the pine cone open, it

cypress (*Cupressus*) and parasol pines (*Pinus pinea*) in Italy

red berries of the common yew (*Taxus baccata*)

scotch pine cone (*Pinus sylvestris*)

releases seeds. The seeds fall to the ground and germinate, producing a new tree.

Ginkgos, cycads, and welwitschia

With more than 48,000 fossil species recorded, it is known that 200 million years ago the gymnosperm group included a great number of species. Nowadays, no more than 600 to 700 species survive. Apart from the conifers, three ancient groups of gymnosperms remain. The first group includes a single species, the ginkgo (*Ginkgo biloba*), also called the maidenhair tree. Native to central China, this tree has large fan-shaped leaves that are shed in winter. The second group comprises the cycads, trees of tropical regions that look like palm trees. The third group is the welwitschia (*Welwitschia mirabilis*). This plant lives up to 1,000 years, yet reaches no more than 10 cm (4 in) in height, although its stem can exceed 1 m (39 in) in diameter.

The ginkgo

A sacred tree in China, *Ginkgo biloba* (above) has decorative yellowish-green foliage, which turns golden yellow in the fall. The photograph shows its plumlike fruit, which grows in summer and falls in autumn.

A cycad

The cycad *Cycas revoluta*, or sago palm, is another very ancient gymnosperm. Native to Japan and China, it has a short, stocky trunk. Palmlike leaves surround the bud, which produces the cone.

17

The flowering plants

- **angiosperm:** a flowering plant.
- **cotyledon:** first leaf of the embryo contained in the seed of a flowering plant. It serves as a nutrient store.
- **dicotyledon:** flowering plant with a seed containing two cotyledons.
- **epiphyte:** a plant that lives on another plant without parasitizing it.
- **gamete:** male or female reproductive cell, which can join with a gamete of the opposite sex to form a new living organism.
- **monocotyledon:** flowering plant with a seed containing a single cotyledon.
- **photosynthesis:** process by which plants, using chlorophyll, produce their nutrients by absorbing carbon dioxide from the air and giving off oxygen.
- **pistil:** female organ of the flower, which receives pollen.
- **pollen:** mass of small grains produced by the stamens of a flower and used in its reproduction.
- **stamen:** male organ of a flower, which produces and holds the pollen.
- **stigma:** upper part of the pistil that collects pollen.
- **style:** column surmounting the ovary and supporting stigmas at its tip.

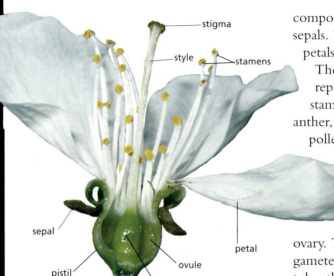

cross section of the flower of the cherry (*Prunus cerasus*)

The flowering plants emerged on Earth during the dinosaur age, more than 100 million years ago. Like ferns and conifers, these plants have roots, stems, and leaves, but unlike them, they have flowers. The flower is not a simple ornament but an essential organ in the process of plant reproduction. Thanks to the efficiency of this reproduction method, flowering plants have gradually come to dominate the plant kingdom. They now represent more than two-thirds of plant species.

The flower's role

The flower is a reproduction organ. The flower produces the male and female **gametes**, the reproductive cells. A typical flower, such as that of the cherry tree (above), is made up of four elements arranged in a circle: the calyx, the corolla, the stamens, and the pistil. The cup-shaped calyx is located at the base of the petals and is composed of five small green leaves, the sepals. The sepals surround a group of white petals (up to five) that form the corolla. The corolla encircles the male reproductive organs, the **stamens**. Each stamen includes a filament topped with an anther, a sac full of pollen grains. Inside each pollen grain are two male gametes. Finally, in the center of the flower is the female reproductive organ, the **pistil**. The pistil is shaped like a bottle, with an inflated and hollow base, the ovary. The ovary contains two female gametes, or ovules, and lengthens into a small tube, the **style**, ending in a protuberance called the **stigma**. Wheat flowers are very different. They are green and almost invisible, with neither sepals nor petals. They have only stamens and a pistil, the two essential elements of a flower.

From the flower to fruit

For male and female gametes to meet and for plant reproduction to happen, pollen must generally be transported from one flower to the pistil of another. This process is called pollination and is carried out mainly by the wind and by insects. In the case of the cherry tree, bees are the pollinators. In spring, when bees visit the flowers, pollen grains stick to their bodies and so are carried from one flower to another. When a pollen grain falls onto a flower stigma, it germinates, producing a tube known as the pollen tube, which grows down through the style to reach an ovule. The male gametes, released at the tip of the pollen tube, then fuse with the female gametes in the ovule. Fertilization takes place, leading to the formation of two new cells and the first stage of the seed. The seed, or kernel, enclosed in the cherry-stone,

water lilies (*Nymphea*)

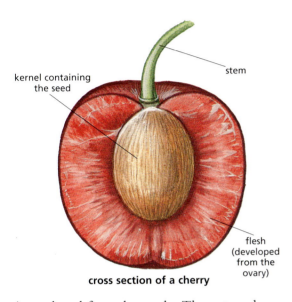

kernel containing the seed

stem

flesh (developed from the ovary)

cross section of a cherry

is produced from the ovule. The external part of the cherry (the flesh) comes from the pistil.

In all flowering plants, the seeds are enclosed in the fruit, and the ovules in a cavity of the ovary. This is why they are called **angiosperms** (from Greek words meaning "boxed seeds"), contrasting with gymnosperms such as the conifers, which are plants with naked seeds.

Two large groups

Botanists classify flowering plants in two groups. Those plants with a single **cotyledon** (the seed leaf containing a nutrient store) are called **monocotyledons**. These are usually small plants such as cereals and grasses, but some flowers such as tulips and orchids and even some trees such as palms are monocotyledons. Other flowering plants produce seeds with two cotyledons: these are the **dicotyledons**. Fruit trees (the cherry, for example), forest and woodland trees (such as oak, willow, and plane), and numerous shrubs form part of this category. Flowering plants have varying life spans. Some live for only one year (annuals) and others for several years (perennials). ☐

A monocotyledon leaf

The flowering plants of the monocotyledon group, such as the iris (*Iris*) above, have narrow leaves that usually point upward and have parallel veins.

A dicotyledon leaf

The dicotyledons, like the cherry tree (*Prunus cerasus*) below, have broader leaves, with a principal vein and secondary branching veins.

As it collects nectar, this bumblebee carries pollen grains from flower to flower.

A composite flower

Flowers are the reproductive organs of most plants, attracting insects by their bright colors. The composite flowers, such as this gazania (*Gazania splendens*) native to Cape Province, South Africa, are in fact made up of small interwoven flowers. Some in the center of the flower are brownish colored and tube-shaped. Others are like yellowish-orange petals with black and white patches at their base. Proteas (*Protea*) are also native to South Africa. They have clustered flowers that create a display of color that looks almost like fireworks (above, inset).

a wild grass: fescue (*Festuca*)

Cereals and grasses

The bamboos

These giant gramineae form forests in China and other wet tropical regions. Some species, for example *Phyllostachys aurea* (above), can reach 40 m (about 130 ft) in height.

The banana tree

Although it looks like a tree (and can grow to a height of 10 m, or 33 ft), the banana tree (*Musa*) is a giant grass. It is topped by long leaves and yields fruit in clusters.

One of the largest families of the **monocotyledon** group is the gramineae, to which most cereals and grasses belong. Cereals are cultivated gramineae and grasses are wild gramineae. These plants, which are in most cases small, have fragile stems and tiny flowers. Many animals feed on grasses, while cereals have become a staple food for people.

A typical cereal: wheat

Cereals are cultivated in all parts of the world. Each continent has a characteristic cereal: rice in Asia, corn in America, sorghum in Africa. In Europe, the most

detail of an ear of wheat (*Triticum*)

beards or awn

spikelet (small group of flowers)

stem

widespread cereal is wheat. Its stem (or straw) is cylindrical and hollow, except at swellings, known as "nodes," from which the leaves sprout. The leaves are ribbon-shaped and have parallel veins. The stem and leaves contain silicon (a substance also found in glass), which makes them hard and sharp. Its little flowers lack petals, but each contains three **stamens** and a **pistil**. The flowers are clustered in spicules, which are themselves grouped to form ears. The spicules are enclosed in cases, which at first are green and later turn yellow. These cases are called glumes and glumellas, which lengthen into long, thin, and stiff hairs, the beards. The abundant **pollen** is contained in the stamens and is spread by the wind from one flower to another. After germination of the pollen on the pistils, the flowers change into "grains" of wheat. The grains are in fact the fruit of the wheat.

Grasses

The noncultivated gramineae, commonly called grasses, form the basic plant cover of the world's prairies, savannas, and steppes. Grass is eaten by grazing animals: domesticated sheep, cows, and others, and wild creatures such as deer, antelope, and zebras. Grasses can be various sizes. In temperate regions, there are small tufted plants like couch grass, fescue, and meadow grass. In warm countries, some grasses such as sugar cane or bamboo reach giant size. Other plants resemble gramineae but belong to related families. Examples are rushes (Juncaceae family) which grow in wet habitats, or even the banana tree (Musaceae family).

a field of tulips (*Tulipa*)

The lily family and the orchids

This orchid (*Phalaenopsis*), native to the tropics, is now grown in many parts of the world.

The Liliaceae family includes ornamental plants such as tulips, lilies of the valley, and wood hyacinth, and vegetables such as garlic, onion, and asparagus. Orchids are especially well known and appreciated for their beauty. These two plant families are monocotyledons, like the gramineae, but their flowers are much more beautiful and colorful.

A typical liliaceae: the tulip

Like many other liliaceae, the tulip grows from a bulb formed of thick leaves, resembling scales, packed inside one another. Set in the middle of the bulb, the bud produces elongated leaves and a stem bearing a single large flower. The leaves and the stem die at the approach of winter, but the bulb lives underground and in the following spring produces a new stem, leaves, and flower. The tulip bulb can

live for several years and so is classified among perennial plants.

A tulip flower has three sepals and three petals, of the same shape and color; six **stamens**, arranged in two ranks of three; and a **pistil**. This arrangement around an axis, like the spokes of a wheel, is characteristic of liliaceae. Most plants of this family are of a similar size to the tulip, but some, like the yucca, grow into shrubs. Some species, such as the lily of the valley and the asparagus, have an underground stem, or rhizome, instead of a bulb.

The orchids

The orchids form an important family of over 20,000 species. Their flowers are composed of three petals and are symmetrical, made up of two identical facing halves. They have two club-shaped stamens that contain masses of pollen grains, which are called the pollinia. The middle petal, which points downward, is known as the lip or labellum. When an insect lands on this petal, pollen sticks to its body. The insect carries pollen from one orchid to another, so bringing about fertilization. In temperate regions, orchids grow from the ground. In tropical regions, many orchids are **epiphytes**, living attached to trees. □

a tropical epiphytic orchid (*Oncidium*)

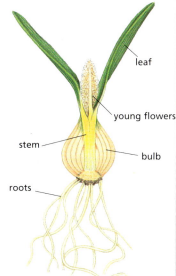

leaf

young flowers

stem

bulb

roots

A hyacinth bulb

At this stage, the bulb (viewed here in cross section) has formed leaves and young flowers clustered at the top of the stem.

The crocus or saffron

Crocuses (*Crocus sativus*) belong, like irises, to the iridaceae, a family related to the liliaceae.

the beech (*Fagus sylvatica*), a tree of the European temperate forests

Forest trees

The common oak

There are more than 400 species of oak. The common oak (*Quercus robur*), below, is a deciduous tree growing to 30 or 40 m (about 100 to 130 ft) in height. It grows slowly but lives at least 400 years. Its bark is used to tan leather, and its wood, which is very hard, for making furniture.

Some nonflowering members of the plant kingdom, including some ferns and many conifers, are called trees because of their size and shape. However, the greatest number of tree species are flowering plants. Most have large flat leaves, which is why they are called broad-leaved, as opposed to conifers with their needle-shaped leaves. Trees that lose their leaves in the autumn are referred to as deciduous. Others that keep their leaves throughout the year are called evergreen. All produce flowers that, after pollination, yield fruits containing seeds. Although they belong to very different families, most forest trees are **dicotyledons**. Palm trees, which are the exception, are **monocotyledons**.

Trees, bushes, and shrubs

The birth of a tree begins with the development of the germ contained in the seed (germination). An oak comes from the germination of an acorn, which is the fruit fallen from another oak. After a few days, the shell of the acorn splits and a stem emerges. This stem penetrates into the ground and branches out to form a root. Then the true stem appears, grows up toward the light and develops small leaves that enlarge and open up in the sunlight.

A tree has three main parts: roots, which anchor it in the ground and absorb water and minerals; the trunk, formed of concentric layers that swell and harden as they age, which is protected by the bark; and branches, which bear the leaves and flowers. A distinction is made between trees, bushes, and shrubs. A tree, such as beech, poplar, or fig, has only one trunk and can grow higher than 10 m (33 ft). A bush is a small tree: it has a single trunk and measures less than 10 m (33 ft). A shrub, such as box and euonymus, is smaller and has several small trunks.

Deciduous trees

In temperate regions, many trees (including maples, birch, several species of oak, beech, and chestnuts) lose their leaves in the autumn. These are called deciduous trees. Oaks, beech, and chestnuts belong to the same family (the Fagaceae) and produce

red-leaved maples (*Acer*) and silver birch (*Betula*)

male and female flowers on the same tree. These flowers lack petals and are grouped in catkins. Each female flower is surrounded by a small cup, or husk, which remains around the fruit that it encases, either completely (as in the chestnut and beechnut) or incompletely (as in the acorn).

Evergreen trees

In temperate regions, some trees such as the holm oaks, which are numerous in the Mediterranean basin, have leathery leaves that are not shed in autumn. They are evergreen trees. In tropical regions, where the winters are mild, many trees never lose their leaves. Examples include some magnolias, native to the southern United States; avocado and bay trees, prolific in Amazonia and southeast Asia; eucalyptus in Australia; guava in South America; mahogany in equatorial Africa; and ebony in the forests of Africa, Asia, and the Americas.

The palm family

Palm trees form a separate family. They are monocotyledon plants, which means that

their seeds contain only one **cotyledon** while the seeds of other trees have two. They also grow in a unique way. Their trunks do not expand in width but only in height. In addition, palms do not usually have branches but bear their leaves, or palms, in a cluster at the top of the trunk. There are around 2,500 species of palm trees. Some, like the date palm and the coconut palm, yield edible fruit (dates, coconuts). Others are used in industry (rattan, raffia).

The chestnut

The chestnut (*Castanea sativa*) has tooth-edged leaves and produces edible fruit. Chestnuts (above) are covered with a hard casing and a husk bristling with thin spines that, when ripe, splits into four parts. This fruit should not be confused with the inedible horse chestnut, the fruit of the horse chestnut tree.

a magnolia flower (*Magnolia grandiflora*)

a palm tree: the coconut (*Cocos nucifera*)

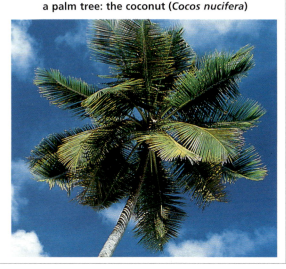

The acorn

The oak (*Quercus*) produces acorns (above). These look like small eggs, sometimes marked with brown stripes, carried in a little cup, the cupule.

25

Raspberries (*Rubus idaeus*) are composed of many small fruits.

The rose family and the legumes

A citrus fruit: the orange

Some plants that yield fruit are neither rosaceous nor

leguminous. The orange tree (*Citrus sinensis*, pictured above) is one such example. It belongs to the Rutaceae family. Oranges are citrus fruits, as are lemons, limes, and grapefruit. In general, citrus fruits have a tough, pitted peel rich in aromatic oils. The inside of the fruit is divided into segments enclosing the seeds or pips. Found in varied natural habitats, citrus fruits grow readily in tropical regions of southern Asia, Africa, and Australia. They are also common in subtropical areas like California and Florida and the countries bordering the Mediterranean, in particular southern Europe.

Among the many families of flowering plants, the Rosaceae and Leguminosae are outstanding. As producers of fruits and legumes, these plants are basic elements of our food supply. Botanists give special definitions to what we commonly call fruits or legumes. They define *fruit* as the organ produced by a flower and containing the seeds of the plant. From the botanists' point of view, not only pears but also tomatoes, sweet peppers, and eggplants are fruits. And what the botanists call a "legume" is in fact a particular type of fruit, the pod of the leguminosae.

Most of the fruits that we eat (such as apples, pears, and strawberries) belong to the Rosaceae family, a group named after the

the rose, which gives the Rosaceae family its name

rose. Everyday legumes (including green beans, peas, and lentils) are members of the Leguminosae family. The rosaceae and leguminosae also include plants that are not edible, such as the rose bush. On the other hand, fruits and legumes related to the rosaceae and leguminosae are present in other flowering plant groups: tomatoes and potatoes form part of the Solanaceae family, squashes and pumpkins are members of the Cucurbitaceae family, and citrus fruits (oranges, lemons, and limes) of the Rutaceae family.

The family of strawberries, apples, cherries, and plums

The Rosaceae family comprises plants of many sizes and appearances. These include herbs (for example, the strawberry plant), shrubs (raspberries, blackberries), and trees (apple and cherry). Their flowers always have five sepals and five petals, a great number of **stamens**, and a **pistil**. By contrast, the seeds inside their fruits differ in shape and size from one species to another.

The trees of the genus *Prunus* (for example, the plum and cherry) bear fruits with quite large seeds, such as the stone of the cherry, greengage, or other plums. Rosaceae of the apple and pear group bear fruits with smaller seeds, known as pips. The thorny plants of the bramble group have even smaller seeds, each enclosed in a small fruit. These small fruits are clustered together, like the raspberry or blackberry. The strawberry plant's group includes both cultivated plants (the strawberry) and wild plants like the meadowsweet, or spiraea. The strawberry's tiny seeds are the small grains that stipple its surface. The rose group (roses and dog roses)

the fruit of the pumpkin (*Cucurbita maxima*)

A peapod (*Pisum sativum*) contains several round seeds, the peas.

includes plants that bear cup-shaped fruits. The rose hip, fruit of the rose bush, is not edible.

The family of peas, beans, lentils, and acacias

The leguminosae form one of the largest groups of flowering plants. Nearly 20,000 species have been recorded. Their common characteristic is a fruit shaped into a long, flattened pod containing a row of seeds. Some of these pods are edible, and others are not. The leguminous plants are divided into three families: the Papilionaceae, the Mimosaceae, and the Caesalpiniaceae. The Papilionaceae owe their name to their flowers, which have corollas that look like butterflies (*papilio* in Latin). This family includes beans, lentils, soy beans, and peanuts. Alfalfa and clover, belonging to the same family, are grown for cattle feed.

The mimosaceae (acacias) typically have small flowers clustered in balls or tufts. Mimosaceae also produce pods, but these are not used as food. Acacias, widespread in Africa, and the florist's mimosa (which is in fact a cultivated acacia, native to Australia) form part of this family.

The Caesalpiniaceae have large colorful flowers that also develop inedible pods. An

example is the Judas tree, a decorative tree found in many parks, with pink flowers that bloom in early spring. □

The flattened pods of the acacia (*Acacia dealbata*) enclose oval seeds.

The zucchini

The zucchini (*Cucurbita pepo*) bears elongated cucumberlike fruits. It is a typical plant of the Cucurbitaceae family. This group includes plants with vining stems and large fruits like the cucumber, squash, gourd, melon, and pumpkin.

The potato

The potato (*Solanum tuberosum*) belongs to the Solanaceae family. Neither the fruit nor the seeds are eaten, but rather the tubers or underground stems, seen here in the process of germinating.

cacti crowned with flowers (*Mammillaria fragilis*)

Cacti and other succulents

Stone plants

The Lithops (such as this *Lithops aurantiaca*) are also called "stone plants." Growing among desert pebbles, they are almost invisible except when they flower.

A euphorbia

In dry desert regions there are plants that can easily be mistaken for cacti. Among these are the euphorbias, such as this *Euphorbia cooperi*, which can grow as large as a tree; it has thick but spineless leaves, which it uses as a water reserve.

In the vast group of flowering plants, cacti and succulents are among the few that manage to survive in dry and desert areas. This is because they can store in their stems and leaves the water that falls in these regions in the form of heavy but very occasional showers. To withstand dry conditions as efficiently as possible, most succulents—for example, the cacti—are covered in spines or hairs.

The cacti family

The cacti, which are native to America, form the Cactaceae family. The largest is the Saguaro cactus, which reaches 12 m (40 ft) in height and can store more than 1,000 liters (over 250 gallons) of water. Cactus leaves are reduced to no more than spines, to restrict water loss by transpiration. The stems are filled with chlorophyll and take over the part played by leaves in **photosynthesis**. Cactus roots do not penetrate very deeply into the ground but extend over a wide area in order to collect rainwater quickly from the very

occasional showers. The flowers have numerous petals and **stamens**, and generally open only at night. The extraordinary shapes of cacti make them highly sought after by horticulturists. A single species, the prickly pear (*Opuntia*), produces edible fruit.

Other succulent plants

Some succulent plants found in other dry regions of the world, such as North Africa, look very like cacti. The cactuslike euphorbias, for example, are distinguished from cacti by containing latex, a white liquid which flows from the trunk at the slightest scratch. Africa is very rich in succulent plants. Here grow the Aizoaceae, which have thick leaves containing water reserves; their relatives the Lithops, or living stones, plants that resemble pebbles; and climbing plants with red or yellow flowers (*Mesembryanthemum*).

spiny cushion-shaped cacti
(*Echinocactus grusonii*)

an umbellifer: the cow parsnip (*Heracleum sphondylium*)

Clustered flowers and composite flowers

ray flower

tubular flower

bract

section of a sunflower (*Helianthus annuus*)

receptacle

The dandelion flower

The dandelion (*Taraxacum officinalis*) is a composite flower. Each "petal" contains a flower that, once fertilized, produces a dry fruit with a tuft of hairs.

The foxglove

The purple foxglove (*Digitalis purpurea*) owes its name to the shape of its flowers, which resemble the fingers of a glove. The flowers are grouped in racemes, like grape bunches. The leaves contain a substance called digitalis, used as a medicine for heart conditions.

Some plants do not have a single flower but a cluster of small flowers at the top of their stem. Most typical of these are the umbelliferous plants. Composite flowers are made up of a multitude of small flowers that appear to form one large flower.

Clustered flowers: the umbelliferae

The umbellifers, such as the heracleum, have tiny flowers, clustered in groups of 50 or more in the form of umbels. Resembling an open umbrella, an umbel has five or six spokes attached to the end of the stem like umbrella ribs. Each spoke ends in a smaller umbel, or umbellule, which bears several flowers at the top of smaller stems. The umbellifers are generally small plants. Some, such as coriander, anise, fennel, and parsley, are used for cooking, but others are poisonous (for example, hemlock).

The composite flowers

The sunflower is a typical composite flower. It is in fact made up of a group

of flowers supported by a stem widened at the top into a kind of platform, the receptacle. The receptacle is surrounded by small leaves, the bracts. The yellow external flowers are in fact petals bonded together. These are ray florets. The internal flowers have small petals, merged into a tube—the tubular florets—the only ones bearing fruit and seeds. The Compositae family is the largest in the plant kingdom and comprises three groups: the liguliflorae (salsify, chicory, lettuce, dandelion), which have ray florets only; the tubuliflorous plants (thistle, cornflower, artichoke), which have tubular florets only; and the ray flowers (sunflower, marguerite, daisy), which have both ray florets and tubular florets. □

a Scotch thistle (*Onopordum acanthium*)

The Invert

rate Animals

The animal kingdom:

- **appendage:** articulated and mobile extension forming the legs or mouthparts of insects and crustaceans.
- **bacteria:** general name given to microorganisms, made up of a single cell, that live in decomposed material or as parasites of humans, animals, and plants.
- **cell:** the smallest constituent element of a living organism.
- **invertebrate:** animals lacking a vertebral column, such as worms, mollusks, crustaceans, insects, sea urchins, etc.
- **phylum:** principal division of the animal kingdom or of the plant kingdom, subdivided into classes.
- **protists:** a group that includes all the living species made up of a single cell with a distinct nucleus.
- **radial symmetry:** an animal has radial symmetry when its body is formed of several identical organs arranged around a central axis.
- **vertebrate:** animals possessing a vertebral column. The vertebrates form a subphyla of the animal kingdom with five main classes: fishes, amphibians, reptiles, birds, and mammals.

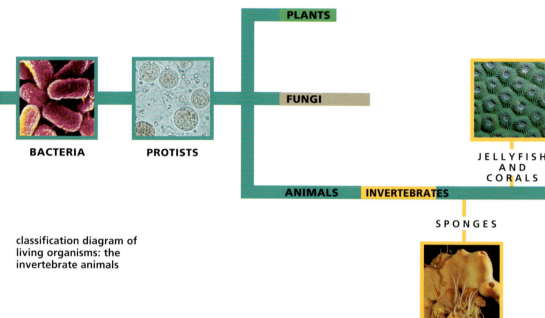

BACTERIA **PROTISTS**

PLANTS

FUNGI

ANIMALS   INVERTEBRATES

JELLYFISH AND CORALS

SPONGES

classification diagram of living organisms: the invertebrate animals

Scientists include in the animal kingdom all animals formed of more than one cell, setting apart organisms formed of a single cell (**bacteria** and **protists**). The animal kingdom itself is divided into two major groups: the **invertebrates**, which lack a vertebral column or backbone, and the **vertebrates**, which all have a vertebral column.

An immense and varied group

Of the 1.2 million known species of animals, more than 1 million are invertebrates. There are fewer than 50,000 species of vertebrates. However, while the vertebrates share a single common characteristic (a vertebral column), the huge invertebrates group includes animals that differ widely, such as the sponges, jellyfish, worms, mollusks, and insects. They are grouped together for the sole reason that they lack a vertebral column. Their diversity makes it difficult to find characteristics common to all these animals. They live in all habitats, on dry land as well as in salt and fresh water. They show the most variety in the seas.

Classification of invertebrates

Since they appeared nearly 700 million years ago, the invertebrates have evolved and diversified continually. Today, some thirty groups or phylums are recognized, of which the principal are the Spongiae (sponges), the Cnidaria (jellyfish and corals), the worms, mollusks, and arthropods (spiders, millipedes, crustaceans, insects), and the echinoderms (starfish and sea urchins). From the most simple to the most highly evolved, these animals have common characteristics within their own group that are used to distinguish them.

- The sponges are the simplest of the invertebrates. They are made up of a cluster of undifferentiated **cells** in which it is difficult to see any structure. Most live in sea water and do not move.
- Jellyfish and corals are also aquatic animals.

red precious coral (*Corallium rubrum*)

he invertebrates

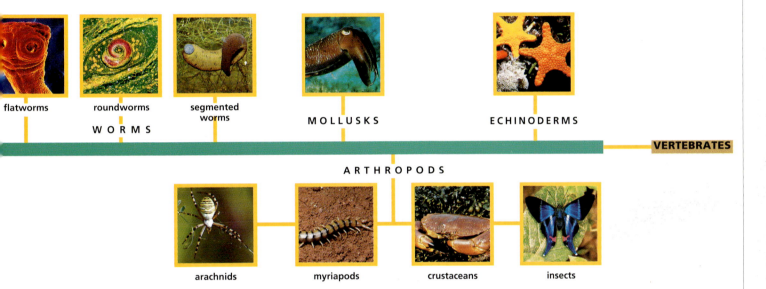

flatworms   roundworms   segmented worms

W O R M S

M O L L U S K S

E C H I N O D E R M S

VERTEBRATES

A R T H R O P O D S

arachnids   myriapods   crustaceans   insects

They have special cells containing poison, which they use to paralyze their prey. Their bodies have **radial symmetry**, meaning that they are formed by a certain number of identical parts (usually five) arranged like the spokes of a wheel around an axis.

• Worms have a somewhat more complicated structure. They have a soft elongated body in which the front (head) and back can be distinguished. This group is now split into several different phyla, of which the most important are the flatworms, the roundworms, and the segmented worms.

• Mollusks, such as the snail, oyster, or cuttlefish, have a soft body, which is almost always protected by a calcareous shell.

• The arthropods form the largest animal group. They have a body formed of a series of rings, or segments. Each segment is enclosed by a rigid case. To this case are attached articulated **appendages** that either form the legs or the organs used for gathering food. This explains the name

arthropod, which means "with jointed feet." The arthropods include four principal groups: the arachnids (spiders, scorpions, and mites), the myriapods (or millipedes), the crustaceans, and the insects, the most numerous group of all with 750,000 recorded species.

• The sea urchins and sea stars are grouped under the name echinoderms, meaning "spiny-skinned," and are marine animals. Like jellyfish and corals, they have radial symmetry. Their body is formed of five identical parts arranged around an axis. They are the most highly evolved of the invertebrates.   □

Early animals

Some of the first representatives of the animal kingdom appeared 680 to 650 million years ago. Fossils this old have been found in Ediacara (southern Australia) in the sediments of an ancient sea. This imprint, 6.5 cm (2.5 in) in diameter, belongs to an animal (*Dicksonia costata*) related to the aquatic flatworms and perhaps their ancestor.

Sponges, jellyfish, and corals are the most primitive animals. They evolved more than 700 million years ago. Their simple anatomy differs from that of all the other invertebrates.

Sponges, jellyfish,

Despite their strange shapes, sponges are animals. They are made up of a mass of undifferentiated cells contained in one or more sacs perforated by small holes or pores. The cnidarians, which include the jellyfish, corals, hydras, and sea anemones, have, like the sponges, a saclike shape. They possess a single orifice that serves as both mouth and anus. On their exterior, they have **tentacles** bearing cells filled with a poisonous liquid. In this liquid there is a threadlike spine, a sort of miniature harpoon, which the animals can extend to paralyze and capture their prey. The cnidarians have two different ways of life. Jellyfish move about by swimming. Corals, hydras, and sea anemones live

attached to a support, such as a rock. They are known as **polyps**.

The sponges

Sponges are strange animals. They cannot move and do not react when they are touched. They live in all the seas, both warm and cold, attached to the sea bed or to a rock. A continuous current of water enters through the sponge's pores, circulates inside, and exits through a larger hole, the **osculum**. This water supplies the sponge with animal or plant debris on which it feeds and the oxygen which it needs to breathe. Sponges have a skeleton made up of independent parts and varied shapes, called **spicules**, a rudimentary nervous system, and reproductive cells. They reproduce either by dividing or by producing eggs by fertilization. The egg transforms into a **larva** capable of swimming. Sucked out of the sponge's central cavity by the current, the larva anchors itself at a distance and develops into a new sponge. Sponges are classified by the composition of their skeleton. There are sponges with a calcite skeleton and others with silica skeletons. Some are made of a less rigid substance: the bath sponge is a skeleton of this type of sponge.

The jellyfish

Jellyfish are made up of a gelatinous mass, in most cases transparent. Of varying shapes and sizes (some are as wide as an armchair), they look like an umbrella with tentacles dangling from its rim. Jellyfish propel themselves by

**a cylinder-shaped sponge
(Verognia lacunosa)**

brain coral (*Hexacorallia madreporaria*)

d corals

a coastal jellyfish (*Chrysaora hysoscella*)

branches of red precious coral (*Corallium rubrum*)

Freshwater hydra

This hydra (*Hydra viridis*) is a cnidarian that lives in fresh water. It uses its foot to attach itself to an aquatic plant.

Sea anemone

This sea anemone (*Urticina lofotensis*) is also a cnidarian that attaches itself to rocks with its foot. It can kill small fish using its tentacles and swallow them in one movement.

contractions of the body, although they will just as often drift in the currents. Most jellyfish live in shallow waters where they find their food, small crustaceans and fish larvae. The poison of some species can be painful and sometimes even fatal. There are both male and female jellyfish. The females lay eggs that are fertilized by male spermatozoons in the water. From the fertilized egg emerges a larva, or **planula**, which floats and then settles on the sea bed where it metamorphoses (changes) into a polyp. This polyp grows and then splits up, producing several jellyfish.

The corals

Corals are mostly formed of a calcareous (limestone) skeleton that protects the living part of the animal, the polyp. Their appearance and their immobility caused them once to be considered plants. Most corals live in colonies. Some, like the madrepores, even build reefs, as their piled-up skeletons gradually form the immense structures known as coral reefs. Reef corals live in a close relationship with microscopic algae. They are found in warm, shallow, clear

waters, in particular in the Pacific and Indian oceans, to depths of roughly 50 m (165 ft). Other species, the brightly colored sea fans, have a skeleton formed of a substance similar to horn, and not as hard as limestone. Red coral is similar. Corals reproduce in different ways. Some produce buds, which break off and form new polyps. Others reproduce from a fertilized egg. This develops into a swimming larva, which then metamorphoses into a polyp. ☐

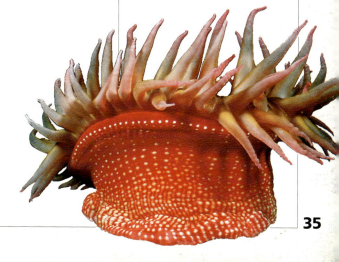

The worms

The first worms appeared not long after the sponges and jellyfish. Although all these animals have in common a soft, elongated body, they belong to several very different groups.

The word *worm* describes a vast group of animals that have as their only common characteristic a soft, elongated body with no skeleton. The three largest groups of worms are the flatworms (platyhelminths), the roundworms (nematodes) and the segmented worms (annelids). The internal cavity of the body containing the **viscera** (internal organs) is not formed in the flatworms. It is still in a preliminary state in the roundworms and becomes truly established in the annelids, which have bodies divided into **segments**. In evolutionary terms, worms are also the first animals in which an anterior section (head) and posterior section can be seen.

The flatworms

The flatworms, or platyhelminths, have a flattened body in the shape of a leaf or ribbon. Their size varies from a fraction of a millimeter to several meters. The main flatworms are the planarians, cestodes, and flukeworms. Planarians are usually colorless and live in the sea, fresh water, or wet environments. Some reach 10 cm (4 in) in length. They are **carnivores** that consume small prey such as fish larvae and insects.

The cestodes, or taenias, are yellowish **parasitic** worms. They live in the body of an animal or human being, and are in most cases harmful. A cestode is made up of a "head" bearing suckers and sometimes hooks that it uses to attach itself to the digestive system of its host, and a series of rings (up to 4,000), which are independent of each other and may separate. Each ring has two reproductive organs: one male and one female. These animals are **hermaphrodites**. A typical example is the tapeworm, which can establish itself in the human intestine and cause unpleasant disorders. Its rings break off in small groups and are expelled with excrement. The eggs contained in the rings can survive outside for a considerable time. If

This segmented marine worm is the fan worm (*Sabellastarte sanctujosephae*).

a flatworm (*Pseudoceros*), which lives in water

The earthworm (*Lumbricus terrestris*) hollows out underground burrows by swallowing soil.

they are swallowed by an animal, for example a pig, they are transformed into **larvae** which burrow into the pig's muscles. Eating the pig's meat undercooked can transmit the worm to a human being.

Flukeworms, or trematodes, which are an elongated oval shape, live as parasites in the bodies of mammals, such as sheep.

Roundworms

Roundworms, or nematodes, are cylinder-shaped. Some very minute roundworms (from 0.1 to a few millimeters) live in the sea, in fresh water, or on land, where they can be very numerous (up to 700,000 in an area the size of a small table). Many nematodes are plant parasites—for example, eel worms, which destroy wheat and beet crops. Others are parasites of animals and human beings. The threadworms and pinworms that live in the intestine are not very harmful, but Guinea worms and hookworms, found in tropical regions, can cause serious illness.

Segmented worms

Segmented worms, or annelids, have a cylindrical body made up of uniform rings, or segments, bonded together. The digestive canal and nervous system cross all the rings from one end of the body to the other. Each ring has hooks, known as **bristles**. Using these, the worm moves across the ground or swims in water. Annelids are classified in three groups, based on the number of bristles found on each segment: the polychaetes, the oligochaetes and the hirudinea.

The polychaetes, which are the biggest group, have numerous bristles. Almost all are marine animals. Some are mobile swimmers, like the nereides. Some, like the lugworms that live in mud, move very little. Others are completely sedentary, such as the fan worm. This marine worm lives buried vertically in sand, in a tube from which it protrudes **gills** that form a plume like that of a flower.

The oligochaetes have only one or two pairs of bristles per segment. This is the case with the earthworm, which lives in underground burrows, seldom venturing into daylight. The hirudinea have no bristles. This group includes the leeches, which feed by drawing blood from mammals to which they attach themselves with their suckers. Leeches live in water but also on trees in the humid forests of Asia. ☐

The threadworm

This roundworm (*Trichinella spiralis*) grows from 1.5 to 3.5 mm (0.05 to 0.15 in) long. It is a parasite of mammals. The female releases larvae that reach the muscles, where they form cysts like this one. Eating meat contaminated by this worm can infect people.

The head of a tapeworm

Equipped with suckers that look like eyes, the head of a tapeworm (*Taenia saginata*) is seen through a microscope and magnified 150 times.

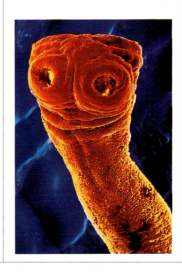

The first mollusks evolved 500 million years ago. Like worms, they have a soft body with no skeleton or legs. Most are protected by a more or less conspicuous shell.

The mollusks

Mollusks are soft-bodied animals, usually protected by a calcareous shell. Their body is made up of three parts: the head; the **visceral mass**, which encloses the various organs such as stomach, intestine, and heart; and the foot, used for locomotion. This body is enveloped by a supple **mantle**, which produces the shell. Between the body and the mantle is a space called the mantle cavity, in which the **gills** are located.

Mollusks are classified into three main groups by their shell type: the gastropods (including snails, winkles, and limpets); the bivalves (clams, oysters, mussels, scallops); and the cephalopods (octopus, squid, cuttlefish). There is a fourth group of primitive marine mollusks, including chitons. Most mollusks live in water and breathe through gills, although the land-dwelling species of snails and slugs have lungs. All lay eggs that hatch into larvae. Many have both male and female reproductive organs. Some mollusks eat plants; others feed on small animals.

The gastropods

There are at least 100,000 species of gastropods. Some (snails and slugs) live on land, others (limpets, winkles) in the sea. These animals are recognized by their single, usually spiral-shaped, shell. Slugs, however, have only the remnants of a shell hidden under their skin or, as in the case of the red slug, no shell at all. Gastropods move by crawling with their highly developed, muscular foot. The whole of the visceral mass sits above the foot—hence the name of gastropod (from the Greek *gaster*, "stomach," and *podos*, "foot") meaning "stomach in the feet." Snails and slugs feed on leaves, while many marine gastropods eat animal and plant plankton.

The bivalves

The bivalves, such as mussels and oysters, all live in water. Their shell is formed of two **valves**, hence the name. The two valves, joined by a connecting hinge, can be kept tightly closed using special muscles, or opened to extend part of the body. Bivalves feed by filtering water for the food particles that they find in it. Their lack of a head distinguishes them from other mollusks.

the scallop (*Pecten maximus*), a bivalve

a gastropod: the grove snail (*Cepaea nemoralis*)

The octopus (*Octopus vulgaris*) is a cephalopod.

Some, such as cockles, venus clams, and razor clams, live buried in the sand or mud. Others attach themselves to rocks, either like an oyster by using one of their valves or like a mussel with the aid of sticky threads that make up the **byssus**. Scallops rest freely on the sea bed and move in a series of spurts by suddenly closing their valves.

The cephalopods

Octopus, squid, and cuttlefish are cephalopod mollusks, living only in the sea. Their foot is located around the head (the name cephalopod comes from the Greek *kephalē* "head," and *podos*, "foot") and is divided into **tentacles** equipped with suckers used to hold their prey. Octopuses have eight tentacles of the same length. Squid and cuttlefish have ten tentacles, eight of which are short and

two very long. Some species living at great depths have luminous organs on their tentacles. The mouth, made of two horny jaws shaped like a parrot's beak, enables the animal to break up small crustaceans and plankton for food.

Although some primitive species have an external shell, almost all cephalopods today have a reduced internal shell (to a "pen" in the squid and a "bone" in the cuttlefish) or none at all in the case of the octopus. Only the nautilus still has an external shell. Many of the cephalopods are rather large for invertebrates. The giant squid, with a length of 15 to 20 m (50 to 65 ft), is the largest of all the invertebrates. The brain of a cephalopod is also more developed than that of other invertebrate animals. Unlike other mollusks, they move quickly by squirting out a jet of water through a siphon located at the front of their body. This propels them like a rocket. In the event of danger, they can also release a cloud of ink into the water to hide them as they escape. □

Sea slugs

These gastropods, including *Nudibranchia chromodoris* (above), are distinguished by having no shell. They are brightly colored, vaguely resemble slugs, and swim by undulating movements of their body. Their main food is sea anemones.

The nautiluses

The nautiluses are the only cephalopods with a fully developed shell, divided into several air-filled compartments. These very ancient animals first appeared many millions of years ago and are now represented only by a few species, including *Nautilus macromphalus* (below).

The arthropods

- **appendage:** articulated and mobile extension forming the legs or mouthparts of insects and crustaceans.
- **cephalothorax:** part of the body of some invertebrates, with the head and thorax merged in one.
- **elytron:** hard forewing of some insects that does not beat during flight.
- **larva:** form of certain animals in the course of their early growth before reaching their adult state.
- **mandible:** each of the two mouthparts of certain insects and crustaceans, used to seize and chew their food.
- **metamorphosis:** changes some animals undergo before becoming adult.
- **molting:** shedding of skin.
- **mouthparts:** organs comprising the mouth of certain animals.
- **nymph:** form of some insects between the larva and adult stages. The butterfly nymph is also known as a chrysalis.
- **ovipositor:** elongated organ at the end of the abdomen in females of certain insects, used for depositing eggs in the ground, in plants, or in paralyzed prey.

This trapdoor spider (*Aphonopelma seemani*) lives in tropical forests.

The oldest arthropods known were already living in the seas more than 600 million years ago. The modern arthropods, which number more than a million species, have retained a basic characteristic from their ancestors: their body is covered by a cuticle, or case, which is in fact an external skeleton, or exoskeleton. This cuticle, which varies in thickness, is jointed at the legs. To grow, arthropods must shed and form a larger cuticle, in a process called **molting**. The arthropod body is divided into a series of parts, known as segments. Each of these supports a pair of jointed and moving **appendages** (antennae, legs, or jaws).

Arthropods are classified into four groups: arachnids, myriapods (or millipedes), crustaceans, and insects, based on the type and number of their appendages. The arachnids include spiders, scorpions, mites, and ticks; the myriapods comprise the millipedes, centipedes, and symphylids.

Spiders

Spiders are arachnids. All arachnids have, in front of their mouths, pincer-shaped appendages called chelicerae, which they use to hold their prey. Unlike other arthropods, however, spiders do not have antennae. Their body is composed of two parts. At the front is the **cephalothorax**, which bears the eyes (up to four pairs), two chelicerae, two pedipalps, and four pairs of walking legs. To the rear is the abdomen, which bears the spinnerets or gland openings from which silk thread is secreted. Many spiders, such as the garden spiders and orb weavers, make a web of silk in which they trap insects. The hunting spiders, such as the trapdoor spiders, lie in wait for their prey in burrows closed over with a silk cover. The crab spiders hunt by ambush, hiding in flowers and camouflaged by matching colors. Others, such as wolf spiders, chase their prey. Spiders are generally carnivores and mainly feed on insects. They immobilize prey with poison contained in a gland linked to the chelicerae. The females lay eggs that they wrap in a silk cocoon, which then hatch into young resembling adult spiders.

garden orb spider (*Argiope bruennichi*)

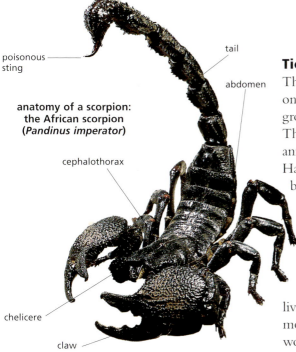

anatomy of a scorpion:
the African scorpion
(*Pandinus imperator*)

poisonous sting

tail

abdomen

cephalothorax

chelicere

claw

Scorpions

Scorpions are also arachnids. They are easily recognized by their two claws and their tail, at the end of which is a sting linked to a pair of poison glands. The sting of some tropical scorpions is fatal. The stings of the yellow scorpion of southern Europe and of the African scorpion are merely very painful. Most scorpions live in hot countries. They hide in cool places during the day and come out at night to hunt locusts, spiders, or other scorpions! After mating, the female often devours the male.

Ticks and mites

These tiny animals (the largest ticks measure only 1 cm, or 0.4 in) mostly live on the ground, in household dust, or on plants. They are generally parasites. Some ticks suck animal blood and can pass on diseases. Harvest ticks or chiggers (*trombiculidae*) burrow under the skin and cause itching.

Millipedes

Millipedes are myriapods (a word meaning "ten thousand feet"). In fact, no members of this group have more than 180 to 200 feet. Myriapods usually live in the ground, because they need moisture. Some myriapods eat insects and worms. Others feed on plant debris. Most are harmless, but some centipedes have two appendages equipped with poison glands and can inflict painful bites. The pill millipedes, which roll up in a ball when touched, are not dangerous, apart from some tropical species that secrete poison. ☐

Harvestmen or daddy-longlegs

These small arachnids (*Pisaura mirabilis*) live in fields, damp areas, and even in houses. Although they look like spiders, they have longer legs and no poison glands. They can deliberately amputate a leg to escape from danger.

A hunting spider

This crab spider (*Thomisus onustus*) is relatively small, and the same color as the flowers in which it hides, awaiting an unwary insect.

The garden millipede (*Julus*) is a myriapod with two pairs of feet on each segment.

a swimming crustacean, the coral cleaner shrimp (*Stenopus hispidus*)

The crustaceans

The green shore crab (*Crustacea portunidae*) is a typical higher crustacean.

Daphnia

Water fleas (above) belong to the order of cladocerans and live in ponds and lakes. They are minute, measuring less than 2 mm (0.08 in) in length. Their body is enclosed in a transparent carapace, through which the female's eggs can be seen.

Copepods

These lower crustaceans (*Eucalanus*) are numerous in the oceans. With their elongated and often colorless bodies, they look like small shrimps. They use their long antennas as oars to propel themselves.

Crustaceans form part of the arthropod group. Their origin dates back over 500 million years ago, and fossils from that period show that they were very small animals. The modern "lower" crustaceans resemble these prehistoric creatures. The larger "higher" crustaceans, such as the crab and lobster, evolved later. Nowadays, 25,000 species of crustaceans are known, and scientists are constantly discovering new species. Most crustaceans live in sea water (crabs, spidercrabs, spiny lobsters) or in fresh water (crayfish) and breathe through gills. Some land-dwelling species, such as woodlice or pillbugs, have organs that resemble lungs. Their shapes, means of locomotion, and ways of life differ greatly from one species to another. However, all species have one trait in common: after mating and fertilization, most of the females lay eggs.

Shelled animals

Crustaceans owe their name to the solid carapace, resembling a shell or crust, that protects their body. They have several **appendages**, jointed legs that they use to walk or swim and claws for gathering their food. They also have two pairs of antennas. Of varying lengths, these antennas are used to detect vibrations, for example, the movements of prey, and to maintain balance. During its life, a crustacean must undergo several **moltings** to increase in size. When this happens, the carapace splits and is cast off, revealing the animal's soft body. Getting rid of its old carapace requires several hours. The body then increases in volume and the membrane enclosing it hardens gradually, forming a new carapace. Many crustaceans, in particular crabs, can grow a new limb when the original limb is injured or torn off.

The lower crustaceans

The primitive or lower crustaceans are extremely small animals, rather elongated in shape. Some species live in sand on seashores all over the world. Others swim in open water, like the copepods. These animals form one of the basic elements of marine plankton and are also found in fresh water. Daphnia occasionally swarm in great numbers in ponds. They are also called "water fleas," because they swim jerkily using their antennas like oars.

The lobster (*Homarus vulgaris*) is a walking crustacean.

The higher crustaceans

The higher crustaceans generally include larger animals, such as shrimps, crabs, crayfish, and lobsters. Their body is divided into two parts: the front, the **cephalothorax**, and the back part, the abdomen. These crustaceans have 14 pairs of appendages, including five pairs of legs (hence their name of decapods, or ten legs). Some move by swimming, others by walking. The shrimps, which are swimming crustaceans, have a light carapace and elongated legs. One of their characteristics is the ability to change color and blend with their surroundings. This behavior is known as protective coloration or camouflage.

Walking crustaceans generally have a thicker carapace and shorter legs than swimming crustaceans. However, they vary in size and shape. Some, including prawns, lobsters, crayfish, and crabs, have claws, while others, such as the spiny lobster, do not. Also, the abdomen of the lobsters, spiny lobsters, and crayfish extends lengthwise, while that of the crabs is very reduced and hidden under a large, flat cephalothorax. There are many crab species. Common species are the green shore crab, the edible crab, and the velvet swimming crab. In tropical regions some species have astonishing shapes and lifestyles. For example, the fiddler crab has one claw much bigger than the other (usually the left), which is sometimes almost as big as its body. The ghost crab shelters in a burrow in the sand and can climb trees. ☐

Barnacles: sedentary crustaceans

Some crustaceans spend their whole adult life fixed to a support. Barnacles (*Balanus*) are visible at low tide, at the edge of the sea, on almost all the world's rocky shores. The animal's body is surrounded by calcareous plates, which form a small cone about 1 cm (0.4 in) high and are attached to rock. At high tide, when the sea covers the rocks, the upper part of the cone opens and thin tentacles called "cirri" protrude. These beat in the water and sieve the fine particles of marine plankton on which the animal feeds.

The ghost crab (*Ocypoda gaudichaudii*) lives in hot regions.

migratory locusts (*Schistocerca gregaria*)

The insects: dragonflies and grasshoppers

The leaf insect

This curious insect (*Phyllium bioculatum*) of tropical regions is a distant cousin of the grasshoppers. It has a large, flattened body with elytrons crossed by veins. This makes it look like the leaves of the trees on which it lives.

The stick insect

Closely related to the locusts and grasshoppers, the stick insect (*Extatosoma tiaratum*) is the longest of the insects: some grow to 30 cm (12 in). It lives hidden among branches against which it blends by changing color (from green to brown).

Insects form the largest animal group, with more than 750,000 species. Like all the arthropods, they have a body covered with a cuticle of varying rigidity and jointed legs. However, most insects also have wings and are the only invertebrates capable of flight. They have adapted to life on land, using small tubes called tracheae to breathe. Insects evolved more than 350 million years ago and spread rapidly to almost every habitat. Only the seas and oceans have few insects.

Insect characteristics

The body of all insects is made of three parts: the head, thorax, and abdomen. The principal features of the head are two eyes, two antennas, and **mouthparts** of various kinds. The thorax is made up of three segments, each equipped with a pair of legs. Many species also have two pairs of wings on the two last segments. The abdomen contains the digestive system and reproductive organs. Almost all insects reproduce from eggs fertilized by copulation.

Insect classification

Classification is based on three main traits: metamorphosis (how the larva is transformed into an adult), the shape of the wings, and diet. There are two types of metamorphosis. In the most frequent kind (including that of flies and butterflies), the egg hatches into a larva known as a maggot, grub, or caterpillar, which as it grows gradually takes shape through successive molts. In this case, metamorphosis is *complete*. In other cases, as

a large dragonfly (*Aeschna cyanea*), its brown thorax mottled blue and green

with locusts, the larva lacks wings but looks like the adult. This is known as *incomplete* metamorphosis.

The shape and arrangement of the wings are also used to distinguish different insect groups. The wings of the palaeopterans (dragonflies and mayflies) do not fold along the body. Those of the orthopterans (grasshoppers, locusts, crickets) fold up like a fan. In the hymenopterans (bees, wasps, ants) the back wings are shorter than the front wings. The dipterans (flies, mosquitoes) have only one pair of moving wings. Homopterans (cicadas and aphids) have two pairs of identical wings. In the heteropterans (bugs), the rigid front wings cover the back wings but not the abdomen, while in the coleopterans (ladybirds, beetles), the forewings form a sheath completely covering the abdomen. Lepidopterans (butterflies) have two pairs of large wings covered with small scales. Finally, some species lack wings: these are either primitive insects, or ones that have lost their wings such as lice, fleas, and worker ants.

soldier termites (*Nasutitermes*) defending their nest inside a tree

folded wings

rear leg (used for jumping)

head

antennas

thorax

abdomen

ovipositor

anatomy of an insect: female great green grasshopper (*Tettigonia viridissima*)

Some insects have **mandibles** with which they seize and grind up small prey and plant matter. These are the "grinders." However, in other insects, the mandibles are transformed into a probe with which the animal sucks up liquids (such as nectar or blood); these are the piercing insects (mosquitoes) and sucking insects (bees, butterflies).

Dragonflies, damselflies, and mayflies: the palaeopterans

These insects experience an incomplete metamorphosis. The larvae, which live in water, resemble wingless adults. The wings of the adults do not fold. Dragonflies are typical palaeopterans. The adults can be recognized by their large eyes and their slender, brightly colored body. Damselflies are smaller than dragonflies. Their flight is slow and jerky. Unlike dragonflies, the mayfly has three long filaments at the end of its abdomen. Their larvae live in water for several years, but adults live only for a few hours, the time needed to reproduce (hence their other name of "ephemeroptera").

Grasshoppers, locusts, and crickets: the orthopterans

These insects undergo incomplete metamorphosis and have wings that fold up like a fan. Their powerful jaws are used to grind up plants and small prey. They move by jumping and emit sounds by rubbing two parts of their body together. The great green grasshopper has long thin antennas. At the end of its abdomen, the female has an elongated organ, the **ovipositor**, which it uses to lay its eggs in the ground. Locusts have short antennas and the females lack ovipositors. They feed on leaves and stems. Crickets have a comparatively larger head and shorter forewings or **elytrons**. ☐

Termites

Termites (above) are numerous in tropical regions. They are social insects and live in colonies. Some species build high mounds of earth, while others hollow out their nest in a tree or in the ground. A termite colony is made up of three castes: the breeders (the king and queen, the only ones to have wings), the workers, which look after the food supply, and the soldiers, which defend the nest.

The praying mantis

The praying mantis (*Mantis religiosa*) is a relative of the grasshoppers. It holds its forelegs, with which it captures its prey, as if praying. The female is larger than the male and often devours him after mating.

domestic honeybees (*Apis mellifica*) on the honeycombs of a hive

The insects: bees, wasps, and ants

Honeypot ants

Ants of the *Myrmecocystus* genus, which live in the desert regions of North America, have an astonishing method of accumulating food stores. Within the colony, some workers are living pantries, storing honey brought to them by other workers in their abdomens. They become so bloated that the abdomen swells to eight times its original volume. Hanging from the ceiling of a gallery hollowed underground, the ants can hardly move. When the other workers can find no more food outside, they come to suck out the honey stored in the enormous abdomens of these living honeypots.

Bees, wasps, and ants form the hymenoptera, a group of insects that undergo complete metamorphosis. They have two pairs of transparent wings with several veins, although many ants have lost their wings. All these insects are attracted by sugar. Bees mainly feed on flower nectar, while wasps eat fruit and small insects. Ants have a varied diet that includes animal prey, tree sap, and seeds. Many of these insects are social and live in colonies.

Bees

There are many species of bees. Some are solitary and others are social insects. The honeybee lives in nests, known to beekeepers as "hives." Each hive holds a queen, the sole egg-layer, several males (the drones), which live for a short time and whose only purpose is to fertilize the queen, and thousands of workers that gather food and maintain the hive. The hive is packed with wax structures made up of honeycomb cells. One part is used as a nursery in which the larvae grow.

The other part, where the honey is made, is a food store.

The wasps

Many wasps have abdomens striped yellow and black. This is a warning. Females have a poison gland that lengthens at the end of the abdomen into a sting, which can have a very painful effect. Some wasps live alone, while others form colonies with a queen and workers in nests made of chewed plant fibers. Among the thousands of species, one of the largest is the hornet.

The ants

All ants live in colonies in anthills. Each anthill contains one or more queens solely dedicated to egg-laying and many wingless workers that take care of all the other tasks. A small number of eggs hatch into male and female winged ants, and these produce the next generation.

The hornet (*Vespa crabro*) is distinguished from other wasps by its red patches.

firebugs (*Pyrrhocoris apterus*)

The insects: flies, cicadas, and bugs

house flies
(*Musca
domestica*)

Flies, mosquitoes, cicadas, aphids, bugs, fleas, and lice are insects that undergo complete metamorphosis. Their **mouthparts**, evolved into a sort of hollow needle, can absorb only liquids. All are biting or sucking insects and many transmit diseases.

Flies and mosquitoes: the dipterans

The dipteran insects (from the Greek *dipteros*, "two-winged") have a single pair of moving wings. Behind are rodlike "balancers" or halteres, used to keep the animal stable in flight. Flies have short, hardly visible antennae and squat bodies. They suck up liquid food using a proboscis that is thick and has small ducts at its tip. Some flies, such as the female horsefly, bite animals and people. A fly can lay 600 to 2,000 eggs at one time. From these hatch wormlike **larvae** (maggots), which metamorphose into flies. Mosquitoes have long, feathery antennae, a slender body, and long legs. They lay their eggs in water, where the larvae grow and do not emerge until after **metamorphosis**. This is why mosquitoes prefer wet habitats. The males feed on sugary liquids (fruits, for example) and the females on blood. Only the females bite.

Cicadas and aphids: the homopterans

Cicadas and aphids have two pairs of identical wings, hence the name homopterans ("identical wings"). They feed on the sap of plants. Cicadas can grow to 10 cm (4 in.) in length and have larvae that live in the ground. Only the male sings, using an organ for emitting sound known as a "tymbal." Aphids are smaller but very destructive sap-sucking plant pests.

Bugs: the heteropterans

Bugs have forewings that are thicker than their rear wings and of a different shape. The scientific name *heteroptera* means "different wings." Some species live in water, but most are land-dwellers. Examples are the stinkbug, which gives off an unpleasant smell, and the pyrrhocorids or firebugs, which have a red body with two black markings. Some bugs eat plant sap, while others such as bed bugs bite animals and suck blood.

Lice

These wingless, biting insects live as parasites on the bodies of animals and humans, sucking blood with their long sharp mouthparts. Their legs are equipped with powerful

claws with which lice hook themselves onto hairs. Three different species of lice live on humans. The head louse attaches itself to the hair and beard, the body louse lives mainly in clothes, and the crab louse (*Phthirius pubis*), seen here in a photo taken by microscope, lives in the genital region.

North American cicada
(*Tibicen canicularis*)

A weevil

Weevils are insects belonging to the order of coleopterans and form the largest family in the whole animal kingdom (46,000 species are on record). This weevil (Lamprocyphus augustus) is native to Brazil. It has a body covered in metallic-colored scales and is 3 cm (just over 1 in) long. Weevils can be recognized by their snoutlike proboscis, a sort of beak ending in a mouth opening. This beak can be long and thin, or short and squat, and is used to grind up seeds, fruit, and bark. Females dig holes in foodstuffs to lay their eggs. Unlike ladybirds (also coleopterans), which rid plants of aphids, weevils are harmful to crops.

seven-spotted ladybird (*Coccinella septempunctata*)

The insects: the beetles

Dung beetles

The small coleopteran insects called dung beetles (*Gymnopleurus virens*) lay eggs in the dung balls they make. The dung provides a food supply for the larvae.

A weevil

Magnified about 100 times, the head of this weevil (*Rhinastus sternicornis*) takes on a horror-movie appearance. Its mouth is at the end of a long, cylindrical snout or beak.

The beetles or coleopterans (including ladybirds, cockchafers, and scarab beetles) are distinguished from other insects by the tough carapace that covers their back. This rigid sheath is in fact formed from their forewings and hides the rear wings. The coleopterans make up at least one-third of all insects and are of many sizes, shapes, and colors.

Characteristics of the coleopterans

The coleopterans undergo complete metamorphosis. The egg hatches as a **larva** or grub resembling a worm, with or without legs, but always with a distinct head. For example, the cockchafer larva is plump with scarcely visible antennae and short legs. It lives in the ground and feeds on roots for three years. Then it changes into a **nymph**. After a further two months, the larva has become an adult insect ready to fly. All coleopterans fly in the same way. They raise their forewings, known as **elytrons**, which remain opened, and then unfold their rear wings, which alone are used for flight. They trap and crush their prey between powerful **mandibles**, which move from right to left.

An immense diversity

The coleopterans have adapted to a wide range of environments, from seashores to high mountains. Their colors vary greatly and are often striking; ladybird beetles are red and black or red and yellow, and

one cockchafer from Costa Rica, the golden scarab, is gilded. There is also great variation in their sizes and shapes. The largest of the coleopterans is the beetle *Titanus giganteus* which grows to 23 cm (9 in) long, and lives in the Amazonian jungle. In contrast,

golden scarab
(*Plusiotis resplendens*)

some species do not exceed 0.5 mm (0.02 in). Coleopterans have diverse diets. Many feed on plants. Some are crop pests, such as the weevils, recognized by their long "beaks." Others, such as the scolytids or bark beetles, eat wood. Despite their small size, they cause severe damage to forests in North America and Europe. Other coleopterans prey on other insects. Ladybirds, for instance, are very beneficial because they eat a great number of aphids. The carabid or ground beetles, which live among dead leaves, eat caterpillars, earthworms, and snails. The dytiscids are diving beetles; their larvae attack all sorts of prey, including small fish and tadpoles. Dung beetles owe their name to their habit of feeding their larvae with the dung of mammals, which they shape into pellets and bury.

an adult butterfly *(Papilio polytes)*

The insects: the butterflies and moths

The butterflies and moths, the order of lepidopterans, are recognized by their four large wings covered with microscopic, usually colorful, scales. Their proboscis is used to suck up liquids, especially flower nectar. These insects have a complete **metamorphosis**: from a larva or caterpillar, they change into a **nymph** or chrysalis and then into a butterfly. Their life span is variable, averaging 1 or 2 months. However, some can live for a year and others for a few hours only. Males locate females by their scent. After mating, the females lay eggs wherever the caterpillars can find food, usually on plants.

Butterflies

The wings of butterflies are usually more colorful than those of moths. Their bright colors attract a mate or warn enemies that they are not good to eat. Butterflies need the sun in order to become active. Often they hatch, live, and die in the same place. However, some species are migratory, moving from place to place according to the season. The largest and most beautiful butterflies live in tropical regions, for example, the *Morpho* butterflies of South America.

Moths

Moths are more numerous than butterflies, and often smaller and shyer. They are nocturnal, at rest during the day and active during the night, which is when they mate. The female emits a scent, unique to her species, using a chemical substance known as a pheromone, which is carried through the air and enables males to locate her, even at a great distance. Moth caterpillars often have unusual characteristics. The caterpillars of the geometrid moths are known as inchworms, and move over plants in a looping fashion. Pine processionary caterpillars march in spring, following one another in processions, hence their name. Leaf-roller caterpillars live in leaves that they wrap around themselves.

□

From caterpillar to butterfly
From left to right.
1. The larva, or caterpillar, feeds on leaves until it has sufficient food reserves.
2. It clings to a support, then changes into a nymph or chrysalis. Its skin hardens and completely encases it.
3. The caterpillar begins to metamorphose: its wings, its antennas, and its proboscis take shape. The casing becomes transparent.
4. A month later, the butterfly emerges from its old skin.
5. The butterfly dries its wings—this is a swallowtail *(Papilio machaon)*—and is ready to fly.

the Caligo butterfly *(Caligo memnon)*

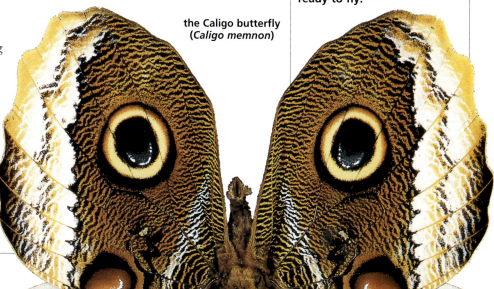

The echinoderms

❂ **bilateral symmetry:** an animal has bilateral symmetry when it possesses pairs of organs that are symmetrical.

❂ **carnivorous:** feeding, among other things, on flesh.

❂ **pedicellaria:** a small pincer, scarcely visible to the naked eye, found in great numbers on the skin of some echinoderms (starfish and sea urchins); these pincers are used for defense against enemies.

❂ **radial symmetry:** an animal has radial symmetry when its body is formed of several identical organs arranged around a central axis.

❂ **regeneration:** natural regrowth of a lost organ.

❂ **tentacle:** flexible and mobile appendage or "arm," sometimes equipped with suckers, which some animals use to capture prey or to help them move.

❂ **test:** hard casing that protects certain organisms, in particular the sea urchins.

This sea star (*Fromia monilis*), resting on a soft coral, lives in the Red Sea.

Crinoids, sea stars, and sea urchins are the main representatives of a group of invertebrates called echinoderms (meaning "spiny-skinned"). Unlike the majority of animals, which have **bilateral symmetry** (or a body with identical left and right halves), echinoderms have **radial symmetry**. Their body is formed of five similar parts, arranged regularly around a central axis, like the spokes of a wheel. All echinoderms live in the sea. Their skeleton is internal, unlike the external skeleton of arthropods. Situated just underneath the skin, it is made up of perforated calcareous plates, from which protrude hundreds of small **tentacles**, full of liquid. These tentacles are used as feet, and the ends are in some species equipped with suckers.

The crinoids

Crinoids are the most ancient representatives of the echinoderm group: fossils have been found that are more than 400 million years old. These ancestors and the species known today, such as the sea lilies, bear a striking resemblance to flowers. Like flowers, crinoids have the form of a calyx that branches out into five long arms. This calyx encloses the various organs. The arms are used to collect food and bring it to the mouth in the center of the calyx. The calyx is attached to the sea bed by a stem growing up to 1 m (39 in) in

purple sea urchins (*Sphaerechinus granularis*)

length. Some crinoids, such as the feather stars, lose their stem when adult and swim freely in the sea.

Sea stars

Sea stars (also called starfish or asteroideans) owe their name to their appearance: their arms, distributed around a central disc, form a star shape. Most sea stars have five arms, but some have as many as 40. When one of the arms is broken off, it grows again: this is known as **regeneration**. The side of the animal bearing the mouth rests on the sea bed, while the anus is on the top side. Sea stars are **carnivorous** animals and attack mollusks like mussels and oysters, opening their shells to consume the contents. To feed, sea stars extrude their stomach, envelop the prey, and digest it. Then the stomach retracts within the body. Sea stars do not swim but move by crawling over rocks, seaweed, or sandy sea beds. There are more than 6,000 species. Some are very colorful, bright red or even blue.

Sea urchins

The sea urchin's body is surrounded by a hard carapace, or **test**, formed of calcareous plates and covered with movable spines that the animal uses to get around. Among these spines are small pincers equipped with poison glands, the **pedicellariae**, which are an

efficient means of defense against enemies. The main organs contained in the test are the digestive tubes and orange-colored reproductive organs. Around the mouth, sea urchins have five chewing "teeth," which they use to scrape off seaweed and small animals attached to rocks. Most of the sea urchins that live on the coasts are round and known as "regular sea urchins." However, some species that live in sand and mud, such as the sand dollars, have a flattened, symmetrical shape and are called "irregular" sea urchins.

Holothurians

The holothurians, or "sea cucumbers," are echinoderms with an unusual shape. Lacking arms and spines, they resemble sausages about 30 cm (12 in) long. These animals live at great depths, in some cases up to 10,000 m (33,300 ft). Holothurians crawl over sand or burrow in the mud, where they digest small food particles. □

The diadem sea urchin (*Diadema setosum*) is recognized by its long spines.

Sea lilies

These strange animals (*Pentacrinus wywille-thomsoni*) resemble flowers but in fact are crinoids. They live in colonies in waters about 2,000 m (6,500 ft) deep. The calyx, which contains the animal's organs, is attached to a long stem and surrounded by ten moving arms. The stem itself stays fixed to the sea bed.

Brittle stars

Relatives of the sea stars, the brittle stars (*Ophiopsila araena*) have long, supple arms attached to a central disc. These arms, which they use for locomotion, can sway like snakes. Brittle stars are widespread in all the world's seas and may live in deep water. They use their arms to trap microscopic plankton for food.

The Vertel

ate Animals

The

anatomical: relating to the anatomy, that is, the form, arrangement, and structure of the organs of animals and plants.

cartilage: organic tissue that is resistant and flexible but not as hard as bone.

encephalon: nerve center made up of the brain, cerebellum, and brainstem in the skull of vertebrates.

gills: respiratory organs of fishes and other aquatic animals.

homogenous: composed of elements of the same type.

oviparous: reproducing from eggs laid before hatching.

lung: principal organ of breath in all vertebrates except fishes.

viviparous: describes animals in which the young develop within the mother and are born fully formed.

Vertebrates owe their name to the main element of their skeleton: the vertebral column. The first vertebrates appeared about 470 million years ago. They were jawless marine fishes.

animal kingdom:

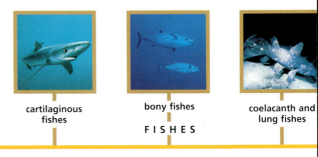

cartilaginous
fishes

bony fishes

F I S H E S

coelacanth and
lung fishes

INVERTEBRATES   **VERTEBRATES**

classification diagram of living
organisms: the vertebrate animals

tortoises

Although less numerous than the invertebrates (fewer than 50,000 species compared to more than 1 million), the vertebrate group forms a **homogenous** group of animals with common **anatomical** characteristics. They owe their name to the presence of a skeleton formed of bone (or of **cartilage** in some fishes), of which the main part is the vertebral column. They all have a nervous system made up of a frontal section, the **encephalon**, housed in the bony skull, and a rear section, the spinal cord, protected in a cavity within a backbone formed by a group of vertebrae. They also have a circulatory system consisting of the heart and blood vessels (arteries and veins), in which the blood circulates to provide the oxygen needed for respiration.

Evolved animals

The vertebrates are the most highly evolved animals and make up almost all the species useful to human beings (who also are vertebrates). They live in every possible habitat, in water and on dry land. The first

vertebrates were fishes, some species of which developed into amphibians. The reptiles evolved from the amphibians. Birds and mammals derived from the reptiles.

Classification of vertebrates

Vertebrates are divided into five main groups, or classes, each characterized by a particular way of life and a special anatomy.

• The fishes appeared first, over 470 million years ago. They are aquatic animals that breathe through **gills**. They have fins rather than legs, and their body is usually covered with scales. The fishes are the most numerous and varied of the vertebrates, with about 30,000 species.

• The amphibians (frogs, newts, and salamanders) evolved from fishes that began to leave the water and move onto dry land 360 million years ago. Amphibians were the first vertebrates to have four legs. The young have gills and the adults **lungs**. Unlike fishes, amphibians have naked skin. Today there are only 3,000 species of amphibians, found mainly in damp places.

Burchell's zebra (*Equus quagga burchelli*)

the vertebrates

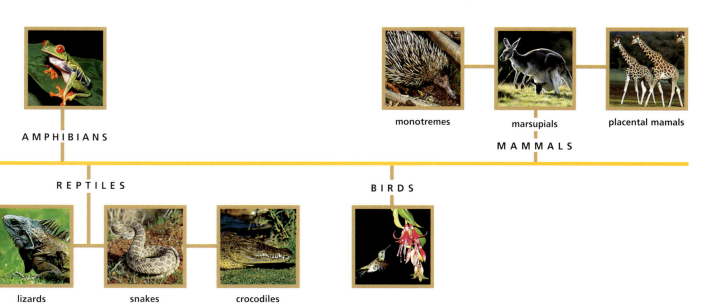

AMPHIBIANS

monotremes   marsupials   placental mamals

MAMMALS

REPTILES   BIRDS

lizards   snakes   crocodiles

• The reptiles appeared about 290 million years ago. Most have four legs, but these are arranged in such a way that they support the body weight with difficulty. For this reason, they move by crawling over the ground. This form of movement is taken a stage further in snakes, which are legless reptiles. Reptiles were more numerous and varied up to 65 million years ago, during the "age of reptiles," also known as the "age of dinosaurs" since dinosaurs were the dominant reptiles of that period. Now there are far fewer, including the tortoises, crocodiles, lizards, and snakes.

• The birds appeared 150 million years ago. An early "bird," archaeopteryx, was in fact a sort of feathered dinosaur, with both reptilian features (teeth and a long tail) and bird features (feathers). Today there are about 8,000 species of birds. They inhabit all environments, including the coldest, Antarctica.

• The mammals appeared just after the dinosaurs, about 200 million years ago. They evolved from curious reptiles known as "mammallike reptiles." However, they did not become numerous and varied until the Tertiary period, about 65 million years ago, when most of the reptiles had disappeared. This is why the Tertiary is called the age of mammals. Mammals are distinguished by a hairy body and the presence of mammary glands that produce milk to nourish the young. Unlike other vertebrates, which lay eggs (described as **oviparous**), the mammals (except for the monotremes) are **viviparous** vertebrates, giving birth to fully formed young.

From amphibians to reptiles

The fossil of this prehistoric animal, *Seymouria*, dates from 290 million years ago. Its flattened skull is like that of the amphibians, but its vertebrae recall those of the reptiles. From such fossils we know that this animal was adapted for walking and probably also for swimming.

The fishes

- **alevin:** fish that has not yet reached adulthood.
- **gill slit:** slit that serves as an opening to the gills of sharks and rays.
- **gill opening:** opening on each side of a fish's head.
- **gills:** respiratory organs of fishes and other aquatic animals.
- **operculum:** rigid fold that covers the gills on each side of the head of bony fishes.
- **oviparous:** reproducing from eggs laid before hatching.
- **ovoviviparous:** reproducing from eggs kept within the body until they hatch.
- **plankton:** a mass of very small animals and plants living in suspension in water.
- **swim bladder:** gas-filled sac, enabling many fish species to hold their position while floating in water.
- **viviparous:** describes animals in which the young develop within the mother and are born fully formed.

The first vertebrate animals were fishes. These were round-mouthed jawless fishes that appeared on Earth more than 450 million years ago. Fishes are very diverse in appearance and form the largest group among the vertebrates. There are more than 22,000 species of fishes out of a total of 50,000 vertebrate species.

Anatomy and ways of life

Not all animals that live in water are fishes. Whales, for example, are mammals. However, all the fishes are perfectly adapted for life in water. To move, they use their fins. They have two pairs, pectoral fins and pelvic fins, on each side of the body. They also have a caudal fin on the tail and, depending on the species, one or two dorsal fins on the back and an anal fin on the belly. The **swim bladder** helps them to sink, rise, and maintain position in water. Only the rays and sharks lack this organ. To breathe, fishes have **gills**, which in most species are covered by an **operculum**. Located at each side of the head, behind the mouth, the gills filter water swallowed through the mouth, extract oxygen from it, and then expel it through openings known as **gill openings**.

Fishes differ greatly in size from species to species. Their bodies are made up of three parts: the head, the trunk, and the tail. The skin is covered with scales, which vary in number and size. On the sides, a visible line called the lateral line is a sensory organ used

This lamprey (*Lampetra planeri*) has a round, suckerlike mouth.

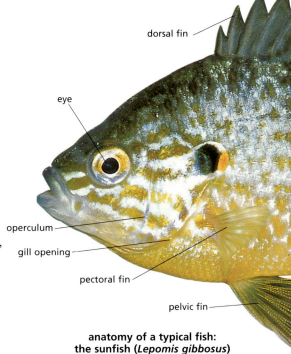

anatomy of a typical fish: the sunfish (*Lepomis gibbosus*)

by fishes for finding direction. In some of the bony fishes, the muscles are separated by small, very fine bones.

Feeding and reproduction

Many fishes hunt for food, which is generally other fishes. Some eat aquatic plants. Others eat both plant and animal matter. Young fishes and some large species such as the basking shark are **plankton** eaters. Reproduction methods vary from species to species. Most fishes are **oviparous**, that is, their young hatch from eggs. The female releases the eggs in the water, then the male covers them with sperm contained in a clear liquid called milt. The fertilized ovule produces an egg in which an embryo develops. The eggs hatch in the water and release small immature fish or **alevins**. In some species, including sharks and rays, the male and female copulate. The embryos then develop within the body of the female, either in eggs (**ovoviviparous** reproduction), or by

caudal fin

anal fin

rainbow wrasse (*Thalassoma pavo*)

these and the more evolved fishes, the teleosts, in which the skeleton is completely bony. Cartilaginous fishes have a skeleton formed entirely of cartilage hardened with calcium. Principal among these are the sharks and rays.

Primitive bony fishes

These fishes, with skeletons formed only partly of bone, are similar to the first known fishes that lived more than 400 million years ago. The most famous is the coelacanth, which has fins resembling feet. Lungfish, found in warm, marshy freshwater environments, also have limblike fins. Relatives of fishes that lived millions of years ago still live in Africa, Australia, and South America. The sturgeon also has primitive features. Instead of scales, it has five rows of bony plates which serve as protective "armor."

A living fossil: the coelacanth

The primitive bony fish called the coelacanth (*Latimeria chalumnae*) has big eyes, a wide mouth, and fins that resemble feet. It lives in the Indian Ocean and until its rediscovery was believed to have been extinct for 60 million years.

The sturgeon

There are 23 species of sturgeons, large and small. They include the common sturgeon (*Acipenser sturio*) (below) of Europe, now rare. Sturgeons are primitive bony fishes that live in the seas of the northern hemisphere and swim up rivers to breed in fresh water. Caviar is made from sturgeon eggs.

receiving nourishment directly from their mother (**viviparous** reproduction). In both cases, the female gives birth to alevins.

Fish classification

The first fishes to appear on Earth had round, jawless mouths. Today only 70 species of these survive, forming the jawless fishes group. Of these, the lampreys are the most well known. They are scaleless and their elongated shape resembles that of an eel. Lampreys attach themselves to other fishes by a sucker mouth and feed on their victim's blood. The other fishes are divided into two groups, the bony fishes and the cartilaginous fishes.

Bony fishes have a skeleton of bone. Within this group are the primitive bony fishes, in which only a part of the skeleton is bone, for example the crossopterygians (including the coelacanth), the lungfishes, and the chondrostei (such as the sturgeon). A distinction is made between

a school of herring (*Clupea harengus*)

The modern bony fishes: the teleosts

The colorful warm-water fishes

This emperor angelfish (*Pomancanthus imperator*) swims in the Red Sea, off Sudan. It is brightly colored, like all fishes living in the reefs of the warm seas.

The lion fish

This curious fish (*Pterois volitans*) lives in the Indian and Pacific Oceans. It has a squat body and a head armed with long spines linked to poisonous glands.

eel (*Anguilla anguilla*)

The teleosts group together more than 20,000 species, the vast majority of the existing 22,000 species of fishes. The teleosts have a skeleton formed entirely of bone and appeared about 300 million years ago.

Features and classification

Represented by species as varied in appearance as moray eels, sole, and angler-fish, the teleosts all have a fairly symmetrical caudal fin and are covered with fine scales (with rare exceptions, including the eels and some carp). Teleosts are divided into several groups. The eel group includes fishes that when young (larvae) look very different from the adults. The herring group incorporates fishes that live in groups (schools). The carp group contains almost exclusively freshwater fishes. The perch and tuna group is made up of fishes with fins supported by hard spikes. They are called "spiny-finned fishes" and make up the largest teleost group.

common carp (*Cyprinus carpio*)

Eels: voyages and metamorphosis

Eels are born as flat-bodied larvae known as elvers. As adults, they have a very long, smooth body, normally scaleless, and a long continuous fin along their back. Eels live in the rivers and lakes of Europe and America, which they leave to migrate to the Sargasso Sea in the Atlantic Ocean, north of the West Indies, where they breed. There, after producing their young, they die. The elvers assume their familiar adult shape during their return journey across the Atlantic. In turn, they too will set out to breed in the Sargasso Sea.

Herrings: life in schools

Herrings live in the North Sea, the English Channel, and the Baltic Sea. Adults have a light-colored belly and a darker blue or blackish back. Like sardines and shads, they live in schools of several thousand. This is efficient protection for individual fish, as one target among many for a hunter. When attacked, the school disperses almost instantly.

Atlantic bluefin tuna (*Thunnus thynnus*)

Carp: freshwater fishes

Several thousand species, found all over the world, belong to the carp group. These freshwater fishes have large scales. Their teeth are fixed not to their jaws but in the throat. The mouth is "protactile," that is, it can move forward to suck up food. The many varieties of carp live mainly in calm river waters, ponds, and lakes in Asia and in Europe. Their shapes and colors differ from species to species. Some have only a few large scales (mirror carp) or no scales at all (leather carp). These fishes do well in captivity. Many varieties have been created by breeders. Carp mainly feed on plants and invertebrates. The breeding season depends on the water temperature, which must not be too cold (20°C/68°F at least). The females lay several hundred thousand eggs, but most of the

alevins that emerge from them fall prey to other fishes, even to adult carp.

Perch and tuna: spiny-finned fishes

The group of spiny-finned fishes emerged about 60 million years ago. With fins supported by hard, sharp spokes, perch are typical of this group. Their large dorsal fin is very spiny. Perch live in the lakes and rivers of Europe and North America. They eat invertebrates and small fishes, including their own young. Other fishes of this group live in the sea, for example, the tuna and the swordfish, two very powerful swimmers that can reach speeds of 100 km/h (62 mph). Tuna weigh up to 500 kg (1,100 pounds) and are carnivores. They are unique among fishes in being able to maintain their body temperature above that of the water. Tuna species include the long-finned albacore of the Pacific and the bluefin tuna of the Mediterranean and Atlantic.

The sea horse

The sea horse (*Hippocampus ramulosus*) is in fact a fish. Whether it is swimming or at rest, it always holds itself vertically. Its body is covered with an armor of jointed bony plates, and its tail is used to hook onto supports, such as seaweed and corals. With its toothless, tube-shaped mouth, it can suck up only very small food particles. The sea horse's method of reproduction is unusual. The male has a pouch on its belly in which the female lays its eggs. It is the male that, after several weeks, brings the young into the world by ejecting them from the pouch.

a spiny-finned freshwater fish: the common perch (*Perca fluviatilis*)

great white shark (*Carcharodon carcharias*)

The cartilaginous fishes: sharks and rays

Sand tiger shark

This sand tiger shark (*Eugomphodus taurus*) has a pointed snout and impressive teeth. It feeds on fishes, smaller sharks, and rays. It can grow up to 3.6 m (12 ft), but despite its fierce appearance, it is not aggressive.

An inoffensive giant: the whale shark

Despite its size and its 3,000 small teeth, the whale shark (*Rhincodon typus*) is not dangerous: it feeds solely on plankton.

Sharks and rays are the chief modern representatives of the cartilaginous fish group, which probably appeared more than 410 million years ago. As their name indicates, they have a skeleton made of cartilage, a flexible material that hardens when impregnated with calcium and is as solid as bone. Cartilaginous fishes are numerous in temperate and tropical seas. They breathe in water through their **gills**, which communicate directly to the outside through several **gill slits** at the back of the head. There are some 550 species of cartilaginous fishes, of which 370 are sharks. The others basically consist of flat-bodied skates and torpedo rays.

Anatomy and life cycle of sharks

Most sharks are powerful swimmers, propelled by a large asymmetric tail fin. (Its higher section is larger than the lower section.) On each side of the body the pectoral fins stabilize the fish, rather like the wings of an airplane. On the back a large dorsal fin, shaped like a wing tip, helps to maintain the direction of the fins' thrust. Unlike other fishes, sharks have no **swim bladder** to hold themselves up in water. Sharks float because their liver contains fats lighter than water. Modern sharks have a mouth opening downward, equipped with teeth that are constantly replaced as they wear out. The

upper jaw is not bonded but merely jointed to the skull, which allows the mouth to open very wide. To reproduce, male and female sharks copulate. In some species, the females lay eggs that hatch in the water. In others, the embryos develop inside the mother, which gives birth to small sharks. Sharks are often accompanied by smaller fishes that follow them or are carried along, attached with suckers to take advantage of food scraps. Although called "pilot fish," these fishes have no role as guides, although some (remoras) may rid the shark of small parasites.

Big sharks and little sharks

Sharks have a reputation for being ferocious and dangerous even to human beings. Although beachgoers must take care on some coasts, especially in Australia and Florida, few species aggressively attack humans. The great white shark can grow to 8 m (26 ft) long and feeds on large prey such as turtles, sea birds, seals, and porpoises. So do the tiger shark of the temperate and tropical seas, and the blue shark, which prefers temperate seas. Another potentially dangerous shark is the hammerhead, with eyes on stalks on either side of its flattened head, which eats bony fishes, other sharks, squid, and octopus. Sharks come in all sizes.

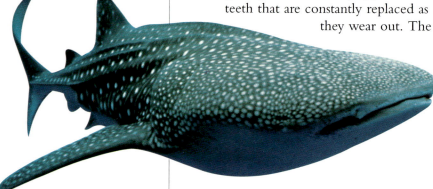

Atlantic thornback ray (*Raja clavata*)

great size, the manta ray does no more than cruise in open water searching for small fishes and plankton to eat. It often makes impressive leaps clear of the water. Some rays are dangerous, however. The sting ray has a poisonous sting in its dorsal fin. ☐

a carnivorous shark: the blue shark (*Prionacea glauca*)

More than half the 370 species are less than 1 m (39 in) long. One example is the roussette, or spotted dogfish, which is caught and sold in fish shops as "rock salmon." The smallest known shark (*Squaliolus laticaudus*) is barely 15 cm (6 in) in length. The two giants are the whale shark, the world's largest fish, which grows to 18 m (60 ft) and weighs 40 tons, and the basking shark, which reaches 10 m (33 ft) and 4 tons. Although large, both these sharks are harmless **plankton** eaters.

The rays

Rays have flat, lozenge-shaped bodies with two large pectoral fins fused along the whole body length. They have big, round eyes and two slits on their head that let in oxygen-rich water, which is then expelled by gill slits on the belly behind the mouth. Their very hard, block-shaped teeth enable them to grind up mollusks, crustaceans, and sea urchins. Rays mainly live in the temperate seas. Normally they stay on the sea bed, flattened against the sand or mud, with which their skin blends. The thornback lives in the Mediterranean and in the Atlantic, to a depth of 300 m (1,000 ft). To reproduce, rays lay rectangular-cased eggs. Most rays are harmless. Despite its

Electric rays: torpedo rays

The electric rays, like this marbled ray (*Torpedo marmorata*), feed on other fishes, which they paralyze with electric shocks produced by organs in their head, just underneath the skin.

The manta ray

Manta rays or devilfish have pointed spurs extending their pectoral fins. This manta (*Manta birostris*) is 7 m (23 ft) across and weighs 2 tons, a giant of the open sea.

About 350 million years ago, animals resembling fishes—but with lungs instead of gills—left the water to take to the land. Their fins became legs. These first land-dwelling vertebrates were the amphibians.

The amphibians

the European alpine newt
(*Triturus alpestris*)

Frogs, tree frogs, toads, salamanders, and newts make up the amphibians, a group of animals that spend a part of their life in water and part on land. All amphibians have the same development cycle. The females lay eggs in water from which **tadpoles** emerge, breathing through **gills**. Then they undergo **metamorphosis**. The gills gradually disappear and are replaced by **lungs** that make it possible for them to live on land. The adults also breathe through their thin, moist skin. This is why amphibians cannot withstand dry conditions. There are 3,000 species of amphibians classified in two main groups: the urodeles (newts and salamanders), which have tails, and the anurans (frogs, tree frogs, and toads), which have no tail. There are also some amphibians that lack both tail and legs.

These are the caecilians, which live in tropical regions.

Salamanders and newts: the urodeles

The urodeles (salamanders and newts) have four short legs of equal size supporting a slender body that ends in a long tail. Their front feet have four toes and their back feet five toes, which they use to crawl. They live mainly in the northern hemisphere. To reproduce, they lay a great number of tiny eggs. Salamanders have a cylindrical tail and spend much of their adult life on land. The black-and-gold common salamander, for example, goes into water only to lay its eggs. In America, some species of salamander live in woods and lay their eggs out of water in the trunks of damp trees.

Newts usually have a vertically flat tail. Unlike salamanders, they spend their adult life in water. Sometimes a distinction is made between the true newts, which inhabit Europe, and the American newts. All newts are aquatic. They rarely leave water or, at least, do not stray far from it. Some live underground in caves.

Frogs, tree frogs, and toads: the anurans

The anurans (frogs, toads, and tree frogs) number around 2,600 species. All have a squat, tailless body, and four legs of unequal size; their back legs are longer than their front legs. They move about by jumping. To reproduce, they lay a mass of eggs that are smaller even than those of the newts and salamanders. Frogs have smooth, wet skin and spend most of their adult life in water. They

South American red-eyed tree frogs (*Agalychnis callidryas*)

common toad (*Bufo bufo*)

are carnivores, feeding on insects and invertebrates. Most frogs of temperate regions, such as bullfrogs, are not poisonous. However, the South American "poison–arrow frogs" secrete from their skin very powerful toxins used by Native Americans to tip arrows with poison. Tree frogs resemble common frogs, but on the end of their toes they have adhesive discs that they use to cling to branches. Flying tree frogs can glide from tree to tree using their webbed fingers and toes.

Toads have dry skin covered with lumps, or warts, which are poison glands. Unlike frogs and tree frogs, toads mostly live on land. Less agile than the other anurans, they walk rather than jump. They feed on insects. The giant toad or cane toad grows to 25 cm (20 in). Native to South America, it has been introduced into the United States and Australia to control insects. In Europe the most abundant species is the common toad. ☐

From tadpole to frog:

From top to bottom:
1. the embryos develop in the eggs,
2. the young tadpoles emerge from the eggs,
3. a week later the tail and back legs appear, and
4. the last stage before life on land; soon the animal will lose its tail.

the bullfrog (*Rana catesbeiana*), which grows to 20 cm (8 in) long

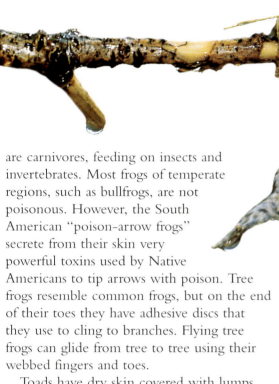

The reptiles

Reptiles were the first vertebrates to live totally on land. After they appeared, more than 300 million years ago, they adapted to the land, sea, and air. Many, like the dinosaurs, are now extinct.

About 250 million years ago, there were many different species of reptiles, including flying reptiles and dinosaurs, which have today disappeared. At present, there are some 6,000 known species, living mainly in tropical regions and in some temperate areas.

Characteristics and classification of reptiles

Reptiles have several features making them well adapted to life on dry land. They have lungs that enable them to breathe air and a dry skin covered with scales that protects them from water loss by evaporation. As they grow, these scales expand, renew themselves, and detach to make way for new ones. This process is called **molting**. Reptiles cannot control their own body temperature. They must bask in the sun to heat up their body or shelter in shade to cool it down. They are oviparous, that is, they lay eggs. Some species, such as the slow-worm and the

adder, are **ovoviviparous**, meaning that they give birth to fully formed young. Modern reptiles are divided into three groups: the turtles and tortoises; the crocodiles; and the lizards and snakes, which make up the largest group.

Turtles and tortoises: the chelonians

The chelonian group includes some 250 species of turtles and tortoises. They have a wide, short body protected by a bony shell covered with horny scales. This shell is made up of two joined sections: the **carapace**, which covers the back, and the **plastron**, which protects the belly. The shell grows throughout the animal's life. It serves as both defense and shelter, because most chelonians can retract their head, feet, and tail. Turtles and their relatives have no teeth, but possess a horny beak for grinding and crushing their food. They are all egg-laying. The group subdivides into freshwater turtles (or terrapins), marine turtles, and tortoises, which live on land.

Freshwater terrapins, like the red-eared turtle, are generally small with a flattened shell. The marine turtles are adapted for swimming, with oar-shaped front legs. They feed on mollusks, crabs, and shrimp. The largest, the leatherback sea turtle (7 ft long and 1,100 pounds), lives mainly in the open sea. Tortoises feed on grasses and leaves and move by walking on their four legs. They can live for a very long time. The giant tortoises of the Galapagos Islands can reach 150 years old.

Crocodiles: the crocodilians

Crocodiles make up the group called crocodilians. These animals have a long, scaly body with a powerful tail and a long snout filled with sharp teeth. They move

The giant Galapagos tortoise (*Testudo elephantopus*) can grow up to 1.2 m (4 ft) long.

the Nile crocodile (*Crocodylus niloticus*)

An Indian gavial (*Gavialis gangeticus*) waiting to catch fish.

A freshwater turtle

This red-eared turtle (*Chrysemys scripta elegans*) has a flattened shell and webbed feet. It is a voracious eater and very quickly grows to some 30 cm (12 in) in length.

Tortoise reproduction

Tortoises and turtles lay their eggs in a hole on dry land and then abandon them. When this baby spur-tailed Mediterranean tortoise (*Testudo hermanni*) hatches from the egg, it must fend for itself.

alligators and caimans, and the gavials, represented by a single species. The true crocodiles are distinguished by their pointed snout and the arrangement of their teeth, visible when the animal has its jaws closed. They live in northern Australia and southeast Asia, in Africa (the Nile crocodile), in Asia, India, the West Indies, and in Central and South America. The alligators and caimans show only their upper teeth when the jaws are shut. Alligators live in the southeastern United States (the Mississippi alligator) and in China. Caimans inhabit Central and South America. The Indian gavial differs from other crocodiles in having a very narrow, cylindrical snout. It feeds on fishes and lives in the Ganges and other Indian rivers. □

across land by walking on their four legs, but spend a great deal of time in water. Powerful swimmers, they use their long tail as both rudder and paddle. Crocodiles copulate to reproduce and lay their eggs on land in a nest of mud and plant debris. The heat needed for **incubation** is provided by the sun. Crocodiles are carnivores that hunt all kinds of animals by lying motionless and almost hidden under the water, showing only their eyes and nostrils, situated on the upper part of the head. A crocodile will seize prey as large as a zebra if it can take it by surprise.

The 22 species of crocodiles are classified in three groups: the true crocodiles, the

American alligators (*Alligator mississipiensis*) spend a lot of time basking in the sun.

an emerald lizard (*Lacerta viridis*)

Lizards and snakes

The flying dragon

This lizard (*Draco volans*) comes from southeast Asia. It is, with the flying snake (*Chrysopelea ornata*), the only modern flying reptile. Using the membrane of skin that unfolds from its sides, the flying lizard can glide from one tree to another.

The lizards (saurians) and the snakes (ophidians) have long, scale-covered bodies and are mainly land-dwelling reptiles. Snakes have no legs, while nearly all lizards have four. Zoologists group them together in the same order, Squamata.

The lizard family: the saurians

Lizards are mainly active during the day and feed on insects and worms. Apart from the marine iguana of the Galapagos Islands, they all live on land. They have long and relatively fragile tails and generally have four legs equipped with claws. Some lizards, however, have only two legs, while others such as the slow-worm have none. Their eyelids can close. During **molting**, their skin comes off in strips. Most lizards lay eggs, being **oviparous**. However, some species are **ovoviviparous**, and the females give birth to fully formed young.

The first lizards appeared more than 180 million years ago. There are now 3,000 species: the true lizards, which live in Europe, Asia, and Africa; the chameleons, native to Africa; and the iguanas, distributed widely on the American continent. The true lizards, for example, the green lizard, have a long body and well-developed legs that enable them to move with great agility. One of their unusual features is the ability to break off their tail to escape an enemy. Chameleons can change color to camouflage themselves. Their tail is **prehensile**, meaning that it can wrap around branches, for example, to give the animal an extra point of support. Their eyes operate independently of each other. Iguanas resemble miniature dragons and usually have a **crest** on their back. Their tail is often longer than their body, and their long toes end in claws.

Classification of snakes

The snakes, or ophidians, shed or slough their skins entirely. They have no eyelids and no eardrums. However, they can detect high-pitched sounds and vibrations through small bones in their head. This is how they locate their prey. Their jaws are flexibly linked to the skull and open very wide, enabling them to swallow (without chewing) animals larger than themselves. The first snakes appeared 130 million years ago: these had four legs and two lungs. Now there are 3,000 modern species, divided into two groups. The first, the primitive snakes, have kept two lungs and their skeletons show traces of their ancestral legs. The advanced snakes have only one lung and no trace of legs.

The chameleon

Like all chameleons, this panther chameleon (*Chamaeleo pardalis*) catches insects by shooting out its long, sticky tongue. These lizards are found mainly in Madagascar and Africa.

the American corn snake (*Elaphe guttata*)

a primitive snake, the emerald boa
(*Corallus canina*)

The primitive snakes: pythons and boas

Pythons and boas are typical primitive snakes and are similar in many ways. They live in trees and hunt by dropping onto their prey, which they suffocate by coiling around them. Pythons are the only snakes to have tiny vestigial back legs and are found only in Africa. Boas are found in most of the world's warm regions. The largest of the boas is the anaconda, which can be up to 10 m (33 ft) long. It is found in the Amazon basin of South America.

Colubrid snakes and poisonous snakes

The colubrid snakes, most of which are harmless, and the poisonous snakes (vipers, rattlesnakes, and cobras), which have special, hollow teeth linked to poison glands, are the advanced snakes. Colubrids mainly feed on rodents. One of the most common, the grass snake (2m (7 ft) long), is found all over the world except in the Americas, in wet habitats. It can swim and hunts frogs and fish. Vipers live in Europe, Asia, and Africa. The most common are the adder and the asp. Rattlesnakes live in the Americas, often in desert areas. Using a heat-sensitive organ in their head, they can locate prey by its body warmth, without seeing it. The snake's "rattle" is made up of horny rings that vibrate when the animal shakes its tail, thus giving warning of attack. The cobras, such as the deadly king cobra (*Naja hannah*), are numerous in Asia and Africa. These are the most dangerous of the poisonous snakes. ☐

The heads of snakes

The vipers, like this asp (*Vipera aspis*), have a flat head with small scales and eyes with narrow, slit-shaped pupils.

asp

grass snake

Colubrid snakes, like this grass snake (*Natrix natrix*), have a roundish head covered with large scales and eyes with round pupils.

A poisonous snake: the rattlesnake

This diamondback rattlesnake (*Crotalus atrox*) lives in the southwest United States and Mexico. When it detects prey, it coils its body and raises its head and neck. Then, with a sudden lunge, it bites the prey and swallows it whole. This snake mainly hunts small mammals.

The chameleon

Native to the forests of Madagascar, an island in the Indian Ocean, is this giant chameleon (*Chamaeleo cristatus*), a reptile 65 cm (25 in) long. It feeds on insects such as locusts and grasshoppers. Motionless on a branch, its very mobile eyes line up its prey. Then, with extreme speed and precision, it shoots out the tongue that resembles a long tube tipped with a club and stuns the insect with a single blow. The victim is held fast in a sticky substance secreted from the end of the tongue. The chameleon can snatch its prey and swallow it by retracting its tongue like an accordion.

The birds

- **brood:** group of birds from the same incubation still in the nest.
- **down:** small feathers that cover young birds and that, in the adults, are situated under the covert feathers.
- **genetic:** relating to genes, elements by which characteristics unique to each species are transmitted from generation to generation.
- **granivorous:** seed-eating.
- **insectivorous:** insect-eating.
- **palmation:** membrane joining the toes of some aquatic vertebrates.
- **rectrix:** bird tail feather.
- **remex:** bird wing feather.
- **sternum:** bony plate to which the wing muscles of birds are attached.
- **talons:** toes of birds of prey, tipped with curved claws.
- **tectrix (or covert feather):** small visible feather covering the down of birds.

Birds are easy animals to identify. Any animal with feathers is a bird, and all birds have forelimbs transformed into wings that they use, in most cases, for flight.

Birds are the descendants of a group of small dinosaurs in which forelegs changed into wings and the body became covered in feathers. The archaeopteryx, which was the same size as a magpie, had teeth, clawed feet, and feather-covered wings. Fossils of this animal have been found in rocks dating back 150 million years. It is regarded as the earliest known "bird," even though it is not the direct ancestor of modern birds.

Anatomy and way of life

Birds are the only feathered animals and, except for bats, the only vertebrates able to fly. Their light, solid skeleton is made of hollow bones, some of which are fused together. To beat their wings, the breast muscles are very highly developed and are attached to a wide, plate-shaped bone called the **sternum**. Flight is aided by the wing and tail feathers. The plumage is made of three types of feathers. **Down** feathers, small and fine, cover almost the whole body and protect the bird from cold. Covert feathers, or **tectrices**, completely cover the down. Third are the large flight feathers, the **remiges** (wing feathers) and the **rectrices** (tail feathers). The color of the feathers often differs within the same species, depending on the sex and age of the bird.

Birds have a beak, not teeth. This is formed of a horny covering over the jaws and varies depending on diet. Birds that eat seeds have a short, powerful beak or bill. Eaters of insects, fish, and fruit have a longer, straight beak. Birds of prey have a hooked beak suitable for tearing up prey. Birds have feet with two to four toes, equipped with

the common cormorant
(*Phalacrocorax carbo*)

tectrices

beak

wing

remiges

retrices

white pelicans (*Pelecanus onocrotalus*)

a parakeet
(*Melopsittacus undulatus*)
in flight

claws used to cling to various supports such as branches and rocks. Birds also have a unique organ with which they make sounds. This organ is formed of membranes in the passages that carry air to the lungs. Air passing over the membranes produces sound. Like mammals, birds have a body temperature that most maintain at a constant level above 40°C (104°F). This has made it possible for them to adapt to all environments.

Bird reproduction

In the breeding season, many birds engage in courtship displays before mating. The females lay eggs in a nest in most cases built for the purpose. The eggs, enclosed in a hard shell, are kept warm by the body of the adult sitting on them as they incubate.

Bird classification

Classification of birds is based on anatomical and biological characteristics, such as the shape of the skull bones, the structure of the feathers, and comparison of **genetic** elements. However, this classification system is constantly changing as new evidence appears. During the course of their evolution, birds have adapted to a great variety of habitats and ways of life. This explains why some species, while close relatives, have very different appearances and behavior. The long-beaked snipe, a wader, looks unlike the puffin, which

has a heavy, brightly colored beak and lives on sea cliffs. The two seem to have nothing in common, yet form part of the same order. Other birds resemble each other because they have the same way of life, but belong to different groups. Thus, the ducks are classified in an order distinct from that of the albatrosses and pelicans although, like them, they have webbed feet. It is often more helpful to distinguish birds by habitat, between aquatic species and land- or tree-dwelling species. The passerine birds merit a section on their own, because their order includes more than half of all bird species. □

A feather

A feather is made up of the quill (or rachis), from which branch filaments or barbs. Each barb divides up into hooked barbules that knit together to form a vane or blade that does not allow air to pass through.

barbules

barbs

quills

feather of the houbara bustard (*Chlamydotis undulata*)

the Indian peacock (*Pavo cristatus*)

Ratites and galliforms

The emu

The emu (*Dromaius novaehollandiae*), an Australian ratite, looks much like the ostrich but is distinguished by its feathered thighs, thickly plumed neck, smaller wings, and three-toed feet. The male, not the female, incubates the eggs for two months. He spends this period half asleep and goes without eating or drinking. These large birds feed on a variety of plants and can cause serious damage to crops.

Over the course of evolution, some birds became adapted for walking and running. Their legs became strong and their feathers became smaller. The ratites, or running birds (ostrich, rhea, emu), have totally lost the ability to fly. The galliforms (chicken, pheasant, turkey, peacock) can fly for short distances but prefer to move by using their legs rather than their wings.

Ostrich and rhea: the ratites

The ostrich of Africa is the largest bird, reaching 2.5 m (8 ft) high and weighing 150 kg (330 pounds). The other ratite species (ten in all) are distributed in various parts of the world: the rheas in South America, the emus in Australia, the cassowaries in New Guinea, and the kiwis in New Zealand. The (closely related) tinamous, which live in the tropical forests of the Americas, are the only ones capable of flying, although they rarely do so. The ratites normally have dull plumage of black, gray, or brown. Their highly developed legs with three toes (two in the case of the ostrich) make them speedy runners. They flee predators, although they also defend themselves with blows from their beaks, legs, and claws. Their basic food is plants or fruit, but they also eat insects, lizards, and small rodents. The females lay eggs, which are in most cases incubated by the male. The male is also responsible for looking after the young. The ostrich's huge eggs are 15 cm (6 in) in diameter and weigh 1.6 kg (3.5 pounds). They are incubated by the male at night and by the female during the day.

Chicken, turkey, peacock: the galliforms

The order of galliforms includes around 270 species. Among them, the best known is the domestic chicken. Galliforms are heavy-bodied birds that fly rarely and badly (except for the quails). On their feet they have three forward-facing toes and a smaller fourth toe pointing backward. With these strong toes they scratch the ground in search of food: seeds, fruit, leaves, worms, insects, and mollusks.

a male turkey (*Meleagris gallopavo*) in display

Many galliform species live in forests, while others prefer expanses of low-growing vegetation. Many have been domesticated: the domestic fowl is derived from a wild species that still lives in southeast Asia. The pheasant and peacock, also native to Asia, have been introduced to other continents as game and ornamental birds. The guinea-fowl, originally from Africa, and the turkey, from America, have become barnyard birds. □

toucan (*Ramphastos tucanus*)

Parrots and woodpeckers

The parrot group includes some 340 species of birds known as parrots, macaws, parakeets, and cockatoos. Because they climb trees easily, they were formerly classified in the "climbers" group, the main representatives of which are the woodpeckers. Cuckoos are quite close to woodpeckers in bird classification, despite their very different appearance.

Parrots

The two basic characteristics of parrots are a hook-shaped beak and feet with four toes in opposing pairs that act like pincers, which they use for climbing trees. They live in noisy flocks in tropical forests and wooded savannas, mainly in Australia and South America, but also in Asia and Africa. Parrots generally feed on seeds and fruit, occasionally supplemented by insects. Some species build their nests in hollows of trees. Others dig burrows in the ground. Their plumage is usually very colorful. Examples include the blue-and-yellow macaw (*Ara ararauna*) and the scarlet macaw (*Ara macao*), which live in the forests of South America. The gray parrot of Africa is less spectacular but sports a bright red tail. Parakeets are smaller than parrots, but their colors are just as dazzling. Native to dry regions of Australia, parakeets are now well-known as cage birds.

Woodpeckers

The woodpecker group has about 380 species of birds. Some have black-and-white plumage; others are very brightly feathered. They are found throughout the northern hemisphere. Woodpeckers skillfully climb up tree trunks, using their four-toed feet (two toes in front and two behind, like parrots) equipped with strong claws, and their long stiff tail as a support. They feed mainly on insects beneath the bark and in dead wood. The bird hunts by hammering the wood with its powerful beak, catching its prey with a long tongue smeared with sticky saliva. To mark out their territory, males tap tree trunks with a drumming rhythm that varies from species to species. The toucans, which belong to the same order, are recognized by their enormous, colored beaks. They live in the tropical forests of America and feed mainly on fruit. □

Pileated woodpeckers (*Dryocopus pileatus*) are skillful climbers.

The scarlet macaw

Natives of South America, macaws grow to 1 m (39 in) in length, making them giants among the parrots. The scarlet macaw (*Ara macao*) is one of the most colorful. Its talent at mimicking the human voice has made it known around the world.

The cuckoo

Cuckoos, like the Old World common cuckoo (*Cuculus canorus*), lay their eggs in other birds' nests. Once it has hatched, the young cuckoo takes over the nest and is fed by its "adoptive parents."

a colony of northern gannets (*Morus bassanus*)

Web-footed birds and waders

The mandarin duck

Native to East Asia, the mandarin duck (*Aix galericulata*) was introduced to Europe as an ornamental bird. It is now found wild in Great Britain. As with many ducks, the males (such as this one) have much more colorful plumage than the females.

The description *palmiped*, meaning "web-footed," is not a scientific term but is useful as a label for several groups of birds living in contact with water: albatrosses, gannets and pelicans, penguins, geese, swans and ducks, and seagulls. Waders, which also live at the water's edge, generally have long legs resembling stilts. Herons, storks, and cranes belong to the greater waders. Plovers, curlews, and sandpipers are lesser waders, or limicolae. The flamingoes with their curious curved bill, long legs, and webbed feet are often classified in a separate order: the phoenicopteriformes.

courtship display of wandering albatrosses (*Diomedea exulans*)

Web-footed birds

Albatrosses, gannets, pelicans, penguins, and ducks all have webbed feet. Their toes are joined by a membrane, the **palmation**. Using its feet as paddles, the bird can move as easily over the water as beneath it. Generally, these birds have four toes, of which only three (except in the gannets, pelicans, and cormorants) form part of the palmation. The albatross has a remarkable wingspan: up to 3.40 m (11 ft) in the case of the wandering albatross! It travels in long gliding flights across the southern oceans and lands only during the breeding season. Albatrosses feed on cuttlefish, squid, fish, and at times on small birds. They drink sea water, eliminating the salt through a gland on their beak near the nostrils. Smaller than the albatross, the gannet can be recognized by its yellow head. It nests in colonies on the cliffs of the Atlantic coast and dives from a great height to catch fish under the water. Pelicans, although clumsy on land, show their expertise as fliers and predators when fishing, which they usually do in groups. They use the large pouch under their beak for carrying fish. Penguins are excellent swimmers but have lost the ability to fly. They use their short wings like oars to dart underwater in search

adélie penguins (*Pygoscelis adeliae*)

of fish, crustaceans, and cuttlefish to eat. They live only in the southern hemisphere, mainly on the shores of Antarctica. (The auks of the northern hemisphere, which look like penguins, can fly.) The largest penguin is the emperor penguin, which grows to a height of 1.30 m (4.3 ft).

The greater waders

The greater waders are divided into the herons and storks and the cranes and rails. Herons and storks have long legs and necks and narrow, pointed bills. They live in marshy areas, where they feed on fish, frogs, and insects. Some species, such as the white stork, make long migratory flights to winter in milder climates. The crane group includes 12 families of birds found all over the world. Cranes are usually large birds, up to 2 m (6 ft) tall, with short beaks. The cranes of the temperate regions (North America, Europe, and Asia) migrate in winter to warmer lands: they fly in V-shaped flocks and punctuate their flight with loud calls.

The lesser waders

These birds belong to the order of charadriiformes. Some species, such as the sandpiper, are no bigger than a sparrow, while others such as the curlew and plover, are pigeon-sized. Depending on the species and season, they frequent ponds, marshes, rivers, and sea shores. Their long legs and elongated toes enable them to wade through water, silt, and mud. Their beaks are designed to catch invertebrates (insects, mollusks, and worms), and take many shapes. Usually they curve downward but sometimes, as in the avocet, upward. □

crowned cranes
(*Balearica pavonina*)

The greater flamingo

The greater flamingo (*Phoenciopterus ruber*) has long legs, webbed feet, and a large, curved beak for sifting small morsels of food, such as little water crustaceans. Carotene contained in the crustaceans gives the bird's feathers their pink color. The mother keeps its young under its wing for about ten days after hatching.

The ringed plover

This small wader (*Pluvialis fulva*) inhabits the tundra of northern Siberia and Alaska. In winter, it migrates to northeast Africa and Australia.

andean condor (*Vultur gryphus*)

The birds of prey

The peregrine falcon

The narrow, pointed wing of the peregrine falcon (*Falco peregrinus*), tapering at the tip, is typical of the birds in this family.

The griffon vulture

Easily identified by its white ruff, this vulture (*Gyps fulvus*) is found in the south of France, Spain, Turkey, and Greece.

The birds of prey, or raptors, are carnivorous hunting birds. All have powerful, hook-shaped beaks that they use to tear the flesh of their prey (small mammals, birds, fish, and frogs); feet equipped with strong, long claws or **talons**; and excellent eyesight with which they can spot prey at a great distance. Despite these similarities, the term *bird of prey* refers to two groups of quite different birds: the diurnal birds of prey, which hunt during the day, and the nocturnal birds of prey, which prefer the night to take their prey by surprise. Diurnal birds of prey have a slim head, ending in a large beak, and a neck that give the bird a streamlined appearance. By contrast, the rounder head of the nocturnal birds of prey is set directly above the body. The eyes of these night birds are specially adapted for seeing in darkness, and their hearing is acute.

The diurnal birds of prey: eagles, falcons, and vultures

Birds of prey that live and hunt during the day are divided into five families. The two main families are the eagles and vultures and the falcons and hawks. Typical of the eagle family is the golden eagle, which lives all across the northern hemisphere, making its nest, or eyrie, in the mountains. Majestic and imposing with a 2-m (6 ft) wingspan, it is one of the most powerful birds of prey. However, it cannot carry off prey as large as stories would have us believe. It mainly catches medium-sized mammals such as rabbits. Some birds of prey prefer to feed on fishes. The osprey, for example, dives into water to catch its prey. The sea eagle shows exceptional fishing skill, snatching and carrying off a fish without wetting its feet!

Falcons and hawks are smaller than eagles. Falcon wings are long and pointed, their tail long, and their beak small and sharp. Hawks have broader wings. The peregrine falcon is the fastest bird of prey, swooping down on its target at nearly 200 km/h (125 mph).

Vultures are not hunters but scavengers that feed on carrion, or dead bodies. Their necks are longer than that of the eagles or falcons, and their head has very short

golden eagle (*Aquila chrysaetos*)

feathers, making it easier for the birds to clean themselves after feeding on a carcass. They also differ in their feet: the toes (three forward-facing and a smaller one at the back) and claws are shorter. They are used for walking rather than killing. The griffon vulture and the lammergeier are still found in

barn owl (*Tyto alba*)

Europe but are in danger of extinction. Some American vultures find carrion not by sight but by using their sense of smell. Among these is the Andean condor, which grows to a wingspan of 3 m (10 ft) and a weight of 12 kg (26 pounds). The California condor is almost as large. It became very rare but was saved thanks to a captive breeding and release program.

Nocturnal birds of prey: the owls

Owls hunt mainly at night. These birds have a large head and a very short neck, hidden by feathers. The feathers of their face form a disk-shaped mask that circles the eyes. The owl's large, round, prominent eyes face the front rather than the sides, as in other birds. The owl's mobile head gives it a very wide field of vision. The Lapland owl can turn its head through almost 360 degrees. Due to their keen hearing and excellent sight, owls can easily find their prey at night. Additionally, their soft plumage is specially structured to give the owl silent flight, enabling it to approach prey without being heard. Some owls have small tufts of feathers on the side of their heads that look like ears. Their brown and gray color camouflages them during the day, especially when they remain at rest. The most impressive owl is the eagle owl, which lives in the hilly, wooded regions of parts of Europe, and in Asia and North Africa. This huge night hunter may have a wingspan of 1.8 m (6 ft). Many other owls do not have "ear-tufts." Typical of the "earless" owls is the tawny owl, which is widespread in Europe, and even found in city parks. It nests in hollows in trees and feeds on rodents. In North America, the forest owl requires a very large hunting

territory, around 500 hectares (1,200 acres) for a pair. The Tytonidae (more than 15 species, including the barn owl), form a completely separate family, the main structural difference being their heart-shaped facial masks. ☐

The tawny owl

Widespread in the forests and parks of Europe, the tawny owl (*Strix aluco*) is recognized by its familiar hoot. It feeds mainly on small mammals, but will take small birds including sparrows.

The eagle owl

The largest European nocturnal bird of prey, the eagle owl (*Bubo bubo*) is capable of attacking a small deer. Like other owls, it spits up pellets containing undigested hairs, feathers, and bones. Its low, guttural call carries over long distances. Once regarded as a bird of ill omen, the eagle owl was hunted and persecuted until it became rare. It is now a protected species.

Young great tits (*Parus major*) hungrily await another mouthful.

The perching birds

The birds of paradise

The birds of paradise are tropical forest passerines that live mainly in New Guinea. The males sport plumage of extraordinary colors and shapes. They display, like this Raggiana bird of paradise (*Paradisea apoda raggiana*), to attract females during courtship.

Sunbirds

The sunbirds, such as this *Nectarinia amethystina*, are small passerines, from 9 to 22 cm (3.5 to 5 in) long. They live in the tropical regions of Africa and Asia. Using their long, slim, curved beaks, they can extract nectar, their favorite food, from deep within flowers.

The passerines or perching birds include 5,200 species, more than half of modern birds. They are mainly perching birds of small to average size, all with four toes on each foot. Many have a vocal organ with which they can produce varied, musical sounds. The great singers of the bird world belong to the passerine order. The suborder of the oscines—by far the largest with nearly 4,300 species—includes the finest songbirds, such as the nightingale, the warbler, and the skylark. However, not all passerines can sing: listen to a crow cawing!

A varied diet

Passerines have managed to establish themselves in almost all environments. Sparrows and starlings were introduced by people to North America and Australia and overran these continents in a few dozen years. This remarkable capacity for adaptation is mainly due to their varied diet. Passerines feed on insects, seeds, fruit, and other plants. Their beak is adapted for their diet: the beaks of the **granivores**, such as the goldfinch or the brambling, is robust and cone-shaped. The beak of the **insectivores**, such as the robin, is more slender and pointed. The beaks of the sunbirds and honey eaters, which are particularly fond of flower nectar, are long, slim, and slightly curved.

blue-tailed pitta
(*Pitta guajana*)

Reproduction

Passerines form pairs during the breeding season. They remain together for the few weeks needed for nest building and reproduction; then they separate. All the passerines build a nest, either on the ground, in branches, or inside a hollow. Some species, such as swallows and weaverbirds, flock together during the breeding season and form colonies that may contain hundreds or thousands of nests. The eggs are mainly incubated by the female, the male taking her place only to prevent the eggs from cooling when she is absent from the nest. Chicks hatch naked and blind and are entirely dependent on the adults for food during their time in the nest. When the first **brood** has left the nest, the female often lays again: some passerines raise three or four broods a year, which offsets the great number of chicks that do not survive.

Great diversity of behavior

In spite of the common characteristics uniting them, many passerines are

gray wagtail (*Motacilla cinerea*)

distinguished by their special appearance or unusual behavior. The woodcreepers, for example, are tree-climbing passerines with long beaks that live in Mexico and South America. The pittas are brightly colored with very short tails, and nest on the ground in the forests of Africa, Australia, and Indonesia. Skylarks are also ground-dwellers, found on the steppes or even in the deserts. Swallows, in contrast, spend most of their time airborne: they usually build their nests of mud. Like many passerines, they are migratory birds. Each year they leave Europe for Africa at the beginning of the autumn and return the following spring. Wagtails never move far from the water's edge and, as their name suggests, constantly wag their long tails. Shrikes impale their prey on thorns as food stores. Tits, often seen in gardens, can hang upside down to reach the small insects on which they feed.

corvidae have also adapted to life near people. Jackdaws, magpies, crows, and rooks can all be found in towns and cities. ☐

The crow group

Of all the passerines, the most highly evolved are the members of the Corvidae family. Crows, rooks, magpies, and jays are the birds with the biggest brains in relation to the total weight of the body. The largest crow is the raven, which can have a wingspan of 1.30 m (4.2 ft). Some species, such as rooks, Alpine choughs, and red-billed choughs, live in colonies, while others like the jay and the magpie make solitary nests. Unlike other passerines, crows pair for life. Inhabiting forests, plains, steppes, and mountains across the entire world, the

A skillful nest-builder: the weaverbird

A close relative of the sparrow is the weaverbird (above, *Ploceus cucullatus*), which mainly lives in Africa, southeast Asia, and the islands of the Indian Ocean. This bird uses its beak to weave spectacular nests suspended in branches. The male takes charge of the work. After choosing his site, he skillfully twists together grass stems and leaf fibers while they are still green. The female inspects several nests before choosing her partner.

The raven

This large, black, crowlike bird (*Corvus corax*) can be recognized by its raucous cry. It is found in Europe, Asia, and North America.

The mammals

Mammals owe their name to the fact that the females have mammary glands and suckle their young. Mammals are the most highly evolved vertebrates. The group has many species, including *Homo sapiens*.

- ◑ **baleen:** strips of horn attached to the upper jaw of some cetaceans, such as the whale, and that filter plankton.
- ◑ **blowhole:** nostril opening of the cetaceans.
- ◑ **caecum:** part of the intestine holding the bacteria that digest cellulose, in some animals.
- ◑ **granivorous:** seed-eating.
- ◑ **hibernate:** to spend the winter asleep or dormant, in a slowed-down state.
- ◑ **mammalian reptile:** prehistoric reptile that showed some characteristics of mammals.
- ◑ **marsupium:** ventral pouch of the marsupials, which protects the young until it is completely developed.
- ◑ **omnivorous:** feeding indiscriminately on diverse foods.
- ◑ **placenta:** organ linking the developing young to the mother's uterus during gestation.
- ◑ **rumination:** method of digestion in grazing animals or ruminants, which use their rumen to store grass. They later bring up the grass to their mouth to chew before swallowing it again into their stomach to digest.

Apart from their principal feature of mammary glands, mammals are also distinguished by skin that is covered with hairs formed mainly of protein (keratin). In most cases, these hairs form a fur coat, but they can also change into spines (in hedgehogs), horns (in rhinoceroses), or scales (in pangolins). Mammals and birds are the only animals able to regulate their body temperature. Evolving from **mammalian reptiles**, the first mammals appeared on Earth at the same time as the dinosaurs, about 200 million years ago. The development from reptiles to mammals was marked by modifications to the skull and jaws, and by considerable development of the brain. For more than 100 million years, while dinosaurs dominated the planet, the primitive mammals remained small and unimportant. When the dinosaurs disappeared, about 65 million years ago, the mammals multiplied and diversified to take over all the habitats and regions of the world.

The four-eyed opossum (*Philander opossum*) has two white spots above its eyes.

There are some 4,600 modern species of mammals. All reproduce by mating between a male and female of the same species, leading to fertilization of the female's egg by the male's sperm. The way in which the young develop distinguishes three groups of mammals: the monotremes, the marsupials, and the placental mammals.

The monotremes: the duck-billed platypus and echidnas

Monotremes are the most primitive mammals: some of their fossils date back 100 million years. From their

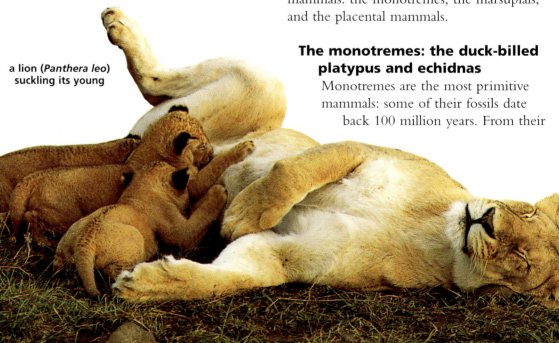

a lion (*Panthera leo*) suckling its young

the platypus (*Ornithorhynchus anatinus*)

The koala (*Phascolarctos cinereus*) lives in eucalyptus trees, feeding on their leaves.

reptile ancestors, the monotremes retain the characteristic of laying eggs. Once the young have hatched, they are suckled like the young of other mammals. Today, monotremes live only in Australia and New Guinea. There are only three species: the platypus and two species of echidnas. The platypus has toothless jaws in the shape of a duck's beak and webbed feet. It is semiaquatic, living in rivers and sleeping on land in a burrow that opens directly on to the bank. It feeds on insect larvae and crustaceans, which it catches by burrowing in riverbed sediments. Echidnas resemble large hedgehogs. They are covered in hair and spines and have a cylindrical snout. Termites, ants, and earthworms are the small invertebrates they feed on.

The marsupials: kangaroos, koalas, and opossums

In marsupials, the baby is born partly developed. It completes its growth outside the mother's body, attached by its mouth to a nipple that in most cases is protected in a pouch called the **marsupium**. There it feeds until it is big enough to lead an independent life. Marsupials were numerous 100 million years ago, but there are now only about 270 species. Some sixty species, including the opossums, are found in the Americas: the others, such as the kangaroo and koala, live in Australia and New Guinea.

The placental mammals

Unlike marsupials, females of the placental mammals have a **placenta** that links the mother to the unborn young and provides it with sustenance. The young are born completely formed and are then suckled by their mother. Placental mammals are extremely numerous and diverse. They are currently grouped into some twenty orders of varying sizes. Classification criteria vary, although they are often based on particular feeding patterns. In this way, a distinction is made between insectivores (insect eaters), rodents, herbivores (plant eaters), terrestrial carnivores (meat eaters), marine carnivores, and finally primates, which are omnivores that eat both plant and animal food. This last order, to which humans belong, comprises the most recent mammals and emerged around 35 million years ago.   □

A giant marsupial: the kangaroo

This red kangaroo (*Macropus rufus*) is nearly 2 m (6 ft) tall and one of the larger marsupials. By leaping with its long back legs, these animals can reach more than 60 km/h (37 mph). Normally, the female gives birth to a single offspring that spends several months completing its growth in her ventral pouch. The young kangaroo continues to take shelter in its mother's pouch at the slightest sign of danger . . . until a new baby takes its place!

a female hedgehog with young (*Erinaceus europaeus*)

Insectivores, edentates, and bats

The shrew

Some 200 species of shrews are known, including this common shrew (*Sorex araneus*) which lives in Europe. Although only 6 cm (2.3 in) long, it eats its own weight in insects every day.

The armadillo

Clad in jointed armor and covered with bristles, the nine-banded armadillo (*Dasypus novemcinctus*), with its movable ears and its tapering head ending in a little snout, is an amazing animal. It lives in the Americas in both tropical forests and desert lands.

The three-toed sloth (*Bradypus tridactylus*) lives in trees, hanging upside-down by its feet. Its call gives the animal its other name, "ai."

The insectivorous mammals feed mainly on insects. They are subdivided into three: the true insectivores group, the edentates, and the bats. The true insectivores are among the most ancient of mammals. They owe their success to the continued availability of insects, which were widespread when the first mammals emerged about 200 million years ago and have since served as a ready source of food.

Insectivores: hedgehogs, moles, and shrews

This group encompasses a range of very different animals, including hedgehogs, moles, and shrews. The smallest known mammal is an insectivore: this is Savi's pygmy shrew, which weighs 2 g (0.07 oz) and is 8 cm (3 in) long when adult. Apart

from insects, the insectivorous mammals feed on invertebrates such as earthworms, snails, and slugs, eating more than their own weight of food a day. They have sharp teeth adapted for seizing and tearing up their prey. Due to the scarcity of insect food at certain periods, insectivores have had to adapt to the seasons. In the temperate regions, therefore, hedgehogs **hibernate** in winter. In general, insectivores reproduce rapidly. The Madagascar tenrec, for example, has 12 pairs of nipples and gives birth to up to 32 young at the same time.

Edentates and pangolins

These mammals either lack teeth, like the anteaters and pangolins, or have teeth unsuitable for biting and tearing, such as the armadillos and sloths. Apart from sloths,

The giant anteater (*Myrmecophaga tridactyla*) is an edentate.

which are leaf-eaters and live in trees in tropical America, these animals eat ants and termites, mostly caught with their tongues, which are coated with a sticky substance. Some species are covered in scales and have extremely long tongues: they include the pangolins of Africa and Asia, and the armadillos of America, which dig into the ground using their long muzzle and claws to find their food. Other edentates are fur-covered, including the sloths, which live hanging upside-down in trees, and the anteaters, which can be recognized by their long snouts and narrow, reduced mouths. The giant anteater grows up to 2 m (6 ft) in length, while its tongue can be as long as 1 m (39 in).

The bats

Bats are the only mammals capable of flight and are found all over the world except Antarctica. Their wings are formed by a membrane stretched between four of the five fingers of their extra-long hands. This membrane is connected to the back limbs and in most cases includes the tail. The fifth finger of the hand bears a claw that the animal uses to cling to surfaces and to help it crawl. Bats often rest upside down, hanging by the fingers and claws of their feet, which are a lot shorter than those on their hands. In temperate regions, all bats, such as horseshoe bats, are insectivores and must hibernate during the winter. They are active at night, emitting ultrasonic sounds and detecting the echoes with their ears, making it possible for them to hunt in the dark. In Africa and Asia,

many bats are frugivorous, feeding on nectar, pollen, and fruit. Fruit bats, or flying foxes, have a wingspan up to 1.5 m (5 ft). South and Central America is home to the vampire bats, which feed on the blood of other mammals. With their very sharp incisor teeth, they pierce the skin of cattle or humans while their victims are asleep. ☐

The giant fruit bat

The flying fox (*Pteropus giganteus*) is a large, dark-colored bat. It is tailless, with large eyes and a doglike face. The clawed fifth finger of its hand can be clearly seen in the picture. With a wingspan of 1.5 m (5 ft), it is one of the world's largest fruit bats. This fruit-eating bat lives in southeast Asia and Oceania.

The horseshoe bats

The greater horseshoe bat (*Rhinolophus ferrum-equinum*) is an insect-eating bat weighing 30 g (1 oz) and common in Europe. The skin membrane, supplied by many blood vessels, joins four of the five fingers of the hands and is attached to the feet, forming a "wing."

the red squirrel (*Sciurus vulgaris*)

The rodents

The lagomorphs: rabbits and hares

Rabbits and hares live in the meadows of temperate regions and savannas and belong to the same group: the lagomorphs. Formerly, they were considered to be rodents and have many points in common with them. Their incisor teeth grow constantly and are continually worn down by their cutting action. However, while rodents have two incisors in the upper jaw, rabbits and hares have four. Hares have ears with long oval flaps, prominent tails, and very strong back legs that make them outstanding runners. Rabbits, like this European wild rabbit (*Oryctolagus cuniculus*), are easily recognized by their ears and back legs, which are shorter than those of the hare.

There are nearly 2,000 species of rodents, representing more than 45 percent of all mammal species. Adapted to all environments, they feed either on grass (herbivores) or seeds (**granivores**). On each jaw they have a pair of incisors that grow constantly, which need to be worn down with regular gnawing. Rodents have no canine teeth, and their molars are covered by especially hard caps, which can grind up grass or seeds. Rodents are generally small. Many have cheek-pouches, which they use for storing or transporting food. The rodent group is varied but can be divided into three broad types of animals: the squirrels, marmots, and beavers; the porcupine group; and the rats and mice, in which lemmings and hamsters may be included.

Squirrels, marmots, and beavers

These animals all have hair-covered tails. They are social and cooperative and active during the day. Squirrels live in all parts of the world except Australia and Antarctica.

The red squirrel is found in Europe; it lives in trees and uses its long tail as a counterbalance when jumping from tree to tree. However, in America and Asia, some species of squirrels are ground-dwellers. Marmots inhabit Europe, Asia, and America: they live in burrows and **hibernate** by living off the stores of fat that they accumulate during the summer. Prairie dogs are widespread across North America, living in colonies. Their alarm cries resemble barking, which explains their name. Beavers, which can weigh from 30 to 40 kg (65 to 90 pounds), are the largest rodents of the northern hemisphere. Using their incisors, they cut down trees to build dams across rivers.

Alpine marmots (*Marmota marmota*) are very sociable rodents.

a brown rat (*Rattus norvegicus*)

a large rodent: the beaver (*Castor fiber*)

All these animals can cause damage to crops and can also spread diseases. Through the fleas and lice that rats carry, terrible epidemics of plague and typhus have been spread across many countries. ☐

The lemming

Lemmings look much like hamsters. There are several species, including this collared lemming (*Discrostonyx torquatus*). In winter, the fur of the lemming turns white and they dig out burrows under the snow.

The porcupine group

This group of animals is mainly found in South America and includes animals as large as the paca, the agouti, and the capybara, all of which are hunted for their meat. Originally from Peru, the guinea pig or cavy is today found all over the world as a pet. True porcupines are found in Africa and Asia, as well as America, but the species differ greatly from continent to continent. In America, they live in trees and eat bark. Elsewhere, they are ground-dwellers.

Rats and mice

Without doubt, this is the most widespread rodent group, with members found on all the continents except Antarctica. These animals are small, large in number, and multiply rapidly. There are many species, including rats, mice, field mice, voles, African jerboas, and kangaroo rats. These are found in various habitats, on or under the ground, in trees, or leading a semiaquatic life in water. Lemmings and hamsters are close relatives of the rats and mice. The golden hamster has become a domestic pet. The common hamster still lives in the wild in much of Europe and Asia.

South African porcupine (*Hystrix africaeaustralis*)

black rhinoceroses (*Diceros bicornis*)

The herbivores: elephants, rhinocerose

The Florida manatee

This strange animal (*Trichechus manatus*) is one of the three modern species of manatee. Together with the dugong, manatees are the only herbivores that are completely aquatic. They are found along the coasts and rivers of America and Africa. The dugong ranges along coasts stretching from the Red Sea to Australia. All these animals graze on aquatic plants, hence their popular name, "sea cows."

The hyraxes

Although small, these rock hyraxes (*Procavia capensis*) are, like all hyraxes, related to the elephants. They have hoofed feet.

With the forming of the savannas and prairies at the beginning of the Tertiary period (60 million years ago), the large herbivores appeared. They evolved in parallel with the rodents, taking advantage of the plentiful plant food that covered the Earth at that period. Herbivores had two main difficulties to overcome. First, they had to be able to digest cellulose, the basic component of plants. This problem was resolved by body modifications. Herbivores developed long digestive tubes, a large **caecum** (fold of the intestine holding bacteria capable of digesting cellulose), and in some species, a special method of digestion called **rumination**. Second, they had to defend themselves from predatory carnivores. For this reason, herbivores are either very large, very fast runners, or live in herds.

Modern species are divided into several orders, formerly grouped under the name of ungulates (or hoofed animals). The number of their toes varies from one to five on each foot.

The elephants

Elephants are the largest mammals living on land. They have five toes on each of their massive legs, which rest on a thick pad. Their trunk is formed by the elongation of their nose and upper lip. It is used for sucking up water to drink and for showering, for pulling up grass or trees, and, since the nostrils are at the end, for smelling. These great eaters and drinkers can consume 200 kg (440 pounds) of grass and leaves and 150 liters (38 gallons) of water a day, yet they have only six teeth: four molars and two incisors, which form the ivory tusks. The ivory trade is nowadays strictly regulated to protect those wild

elephants that still survive. There are two species: the African elephant and the Asian elephant. The habitat of the African elephant is savanna and forest to an altitude of 3,600 m (12,000 ft). It lives in small herds, each led by an old female. The Asian elephant can be distinguished by its smaller size, less voluminous ears, and its generally shorter

The African elephant (*Loxodonta africana*) can move fast, despite its imposing size.

nd horses

tusks. Also, its trunk has a single "lip" while that of the African elephant has two.

The rhinoceroses and tapirs

These three-toed animals lead a solitary life. Rhinoceroses have a hard leathery skin that can be as much as 6 cm (over 2 in) thick. There are five species of rhinoceros, including the black rhinoceros, which lives in tropical Africa and has two horns on its head, and the Indian rhinoceros, which has only one. These horns are greatly sought after, so that rhinos have been hunted until they are now rare. Tapirs are forest animals. The Malayan tapir lives in southeast Asia, and the other species in tropical America. All are the size of a small horse and have a short trunk formed, like the elephant's, by the nose and upper lip.

The horses, asses, and zebras

Horses, asses, and zebras make up the equines, and their chief characteristic is a single toe that forms a hoof. In addition, modifications to their skeleton make it possible

The adult Malayan tapir (*Tapirus indicus*) has black and white markings.

for them to run very quickly over hard ground. All these herbivores live on savannas or steppes. The group was formerly numerous, but now only some ten species exist worldwide. The one remaining wild species is Przewalski's horse, native to Mongolia. All other horses are domesticated, although some species of wild ass (the onager and kiang) still exist in Africa and Asia. Zebras are aggressive and have seldom been tamed. The three species of zebra all live in Africa, including the common plains zebra and Grevy's zebra, and are easily recognized by their stripes. ☐

Przewalski's horse

The last horse to have lived in the wild, Przewalski's horse (*Equus przewalskii*) is probably the ancestor of all our domestic horses. This animal has practically disappeared (only about a thousand survive) and now only lives in captivity. Those in the photograph below live in France in the Cevennes park, where attempts are being made to reintroduce the species to the wild. Native to Mongolia, this small horse was formerly very widespread. It is thought that Przewalski's horse, or a closely related species, the tarpan, appears in the prehistoric wall paintings in caves such as Lascaux. It differs from domestic horses in its brown coat lined with black on the back, its short, bristly mane, massive head, and white muzzle.

European red deer (*Cervus elaphus*)

The herbivores: ruminants, hippopotamuses,

An African ruminant: the giraffe

All giraffes have a pair of horns, which can be 25 cm (10 in) long. Some males develop additional bony protuberances. This giraffe (*Giraffa camelopardalis*) has one such bump in front of its principal horns.

The herbivores called artiodactyls have an even number of toes, either two or four. Formerly classed as ungulates, or hoofed mammals, they include the ruminants (cattle, deer, giraffes, camels), which have a stomach divided into four chambers (rumen, reticulum, omasum, and abomasum) and animals such as the hippopotamuses, peccaries, and wild boar, which have a simpler stomach.

The ruminants

Their complex stomachs allows ruminants to absorb a large quantity of plant matter at one time. They swallow grass as quickly as possible, store it in their rumen, and then move themselves out of range of predators. Next, they regurgitate the grass in mouthfuls, chew at leisure, and then swallow it again and digest. This method of digestion is called **rumination**, hence their name. There are four principal ruminant families: the bovids, the cervids, the giraffids, and the camelids. The bison, yak, musk ox, chamois, mouflon, and all the antelopes (for example, the impalas), are members of the bovid family. These ruminants resemble the wild ancestors of domestic cows, goats, and sheep. All these animals have simple, unbranched horns that are not shed. Elk (or wapiti), moose, woodland deer such as roe, red and fallow deer, and reindeer (or caribou) are among the most widespread cervids. Unlike the bovids, they have branched horns known as antlers that are shed and regrow each year. Normally, only the males have antlers.

Giraffes and okapis belong to the giraffid family. These ruminants live in tropical

Bactrian camels (*Camelus bactrianus*) are the last wild camels.

Africa. They have small, skin-covered horns and spend more than 12 hours a day feeding. The giraffe's long neck allows it to eat young shoots or leaves picked from the tops of trees. They can be solitary but generally prefer to live in small groups. The males often fight. Bactrian camels, dromedaries or Arabian camels, llamas, alpacas, and vicunas are all camelids. They live in arid regions of Asia and in the mountains of South America. The Bactrian camel—which has two humps— lives in central Asia. The dromedary—which has only one hump—is originally from Arabia. Highly adapted to the desert, it has

The musk ox (*Ovibos moschatus*) is a ruminant of the Arctic tundra.

impala (*Aepyceros melampus*)

nd wild pigs

been introduced to the Sahara and other regions of Africa.

Hippopotamuses and wild boars

The hippopotamus of tropical Africa is related to the pig but is much larger, weighing as much as four tons. This animal spends much of its life in water. The position of its nostrils on top of the head allows it to breathe while immersed in water. The female gives birth in shallow water and her young suckle underwater while holding their breath! The hippopotamus eats little considering its size: 40 kg (88 pounds) of fresh grass per day for a weight of up to two tons. Less aquatic than its big "cousin," the pygmy hippopotamus lives mainly in the tropical forest. It has become very rare, for its natural habitat is gradually disappearing, but a few still live in Africa. The wild boar is the ancestor of the domestic pig. In spring and summer, it eats stems, leaves, and grass

flowers; in autumn and winter, it feeds on acorns and roots, which it searches out in the ground with its snout. It may also eat small rodents, grasshoppers, and even small birds. The forest hogs, river hogs (or bush pigs), and warthogs of Africa belong to the same family. The peccaries of America are represented by three species. These are the American cousins of the wild pigs and belong to a related family.

The alpaca

Like the llama, the alpaca (*Lama pacos*) defends itself by spitting. It lives in South America, in mountains up to an altitude of 3,500 m (11,000 ft).

The hippopotamus

With nostrils, ears, and eyes on top of their skull, hippos (*Hippopotamus amphibius*) smell, hear, and see without leaving the water.

The meerkats

Here standing on their hind legs and scanning their surroundings like sentries, meerkats (*Suricata suricata*) like to bask in the morning sun. But the nights are often very cold in the Kalahari desert of southern Africa, where these relatives of the mongooses live. During the hottest hours of the day, meerkats seek refuge in underground burrows that they dig out with their long claws. They are social animals and often show affection and kinship by embracing and rubbing their soft, furry muzzles together.

Bengal tigers (*Panthera tigris*)

The carnivores

The polecat

This small carnivore (*Mustela putorius*) belongs to the mustelid family, like the weasel, marten, and mink. Like them, it feeds on rodents, birds, lizards, and frogs. Its anal glands secrete a substance that gives off a very bad smell.

As hunters of live prey, carnivores need teeth that are specially adapted: fangs for killing, incisors for tearing skin, and molars for cutting up flesh and eating it. Weasels, ermines, tigers, and panthers hunt alone. Lions, wolves, and Cape hunting dogs hunt in packs, making it possible for them to tackle large prey, which they usually share. Foxes, martens, and raccoons are hunters that also eat fruit, eggs, and other foods. Otters catch fish. Bears, except the polar bear, eat mainly plants.

Wolves and foxes

Wolves and foxes belong to the canid family and resemble dogs. Their highly developed muscles and their long legs enable them to run very fast. Wolves formerly ranged across

a female wolf (*Canis lupus*) with her young

almost all of the northern hemisphere, but they have been exterminated in many countries. They live in packs that are hierarchical (some wolves dominate others) and communicate through a range of diverse calls. The fox, which also ranges across almost all of the northern hemisphere, lives either alone or in family groups in dens. It is a cunning animal that has adapted to new habitats. It often forages around city suburbs in search of food, since it will eat whatever is available.

The cats

All members of the family of felids (or felines) resemble the domestic cat, having a short face with fairly rounded ears, five toes on the forelegs and four on the hind legs, and retractable claws. Of all the predators, felines have the most obvious carnivorous traits, especially visible in their teeth: on

A lion (*Panthera leo*) lounging in the shade; it rests for 20 hours a day.

polar bears (*Ursus maritimus*) on the ice-pack

average they have only 30 (dogs and bears have 42), but their canines are large and curved. The domestic cat is probably the descendant of wildcats from the Near East and Africa, where the Egyptians were the first to tame the cat more than 4,000 years ago. Other feral species, small and large, still survive. They include the European wildcat, the puma or cougar of America, and the golden cat of Asia. The lynx is easily recognizable from the brushlike tufts of hair on its ears. This cat does not chase its prey of rabbits, hares, or even roe deer but approaches them furtively before jumping on them. There are two species of lynx in North America, mainly confined to Canada. In Europe, the lynx has become very rare, but attempts are being made to reintroduce it in several regions.

The genus *Panthera* includes four of the "big cats": the leopard or panther, which inhabits Africa and Asia; the jaguar of America; the Asian tiger; and the lion which is found mainly in Africa and in a small area of India. The lion, unlike the other big cats, lives in social groups in which the females usually do the hunting. The smaller cheetah ranges over the African savannas and western Asia and is the fastest land animal.

The bears

Although traditionally included in the carnivores group, bears are in fact omnivores that eat plants as well as animals. Like human beings, they are plantigrade (when walking they place the complete sole of the foot on the ground). Despite their heavy, massive body, they are quite agile and quick. The polar bear is a powerful carnivore of 700 kg (1,500 pounds) and 2.50 m (8 ft) in length. Ranging across arctic regions in Canada, Alaska, and Siberia, the polar bear is an excellent swimmer that feeds on seals and fishes. The grizzly bear's habitat stretches from Alaska to the Rocky Mountains of the United States. It has a reputation for attacking humans and cattle but in fact feeds mainly on plants and small rodents. The European brown bear belongs to the same species but is smaller and less aggressive and has now become extremely rare. The black bear is yet smaller and is found over a large part of North America. It is very agile, climbing trees in search of fruit and insects or to take shelter when in danger. ☐

The panda

The giant panda (*Ailuropoda melanoleuca*), which is now classified among the bears, has become very rare. It survives only in southwest China, living between altitudes of 2,500 and 3,000 m (8,000 to 10,000 ft) where forests of broadleaved trees and bamboos are thickest. The panda feeds almost exclusively on bamboo, which has such a low nutritional value that the animal needs to absorb very large quantities. It spends 14 hours a day eating.

The cheetah (*Acinonyx jubatus*) can outsprint its antelope prey.

Greenland or harp seals (*Phoca groenlandica*)

The marine mammals

A large pinniped: the walrus

The walrus (*Odobenus rosmarus*) is easily recognizable by its two long tusks. Although sometimes used for fighting, the main purpose of these long teeth is for underwater digging in silt to find food. The largest males can be 3 m (almost 10 ft) long and weigh more than 1,000 kg (over 2,000 pounds). Despite their impressive size, walruses move very quickly in the sea. They live in the polar regions, in large colonies sometimes numbering several thousand animals.

The mammals that returned to the sea about 26 million years ago are probably descended from carnivores and ungulates. Some scientists trace their prehistoric ancestors to the otters and others to the bears. Whatever their exact origin, they are thoroughly adapted for marine life. Their bodies are elongated and their feet are webbed and have shortened to become modified fins. However, they have retained the basic mammal characteristics of hair, mammary glands, and a constant internal body temperature. There are two principal groups of marine mammals: the pinnipeds (seals, walruses, and sea lions) and the cetaceans (whales and dolphins).

The pinnipeds: seals, walruses, and sea lions

The pinnipeds are descended from carnivores and feed on fish, cuttlefish, squid, and octopus when available. They are less aquatic than the cetaceans and leave the water to give birth. In many species, care of the young is very short: after about three weeks, the mother abandons the pup, which learns to swim and hunt

the elephant seal of the northern hemisphere
(*Mirounga angustirostris*)

by itself. Their four limbs are blade-shaped flippers supported by very long finger bones. Pinnipeds live in colonies. There are 19 species of seals, including the Greenland or harp seal. Seals live mainly in the harsh climatic conditions of the Arctic and Antarctic. The elephant seal is a giant seal, 6.5 m (21 ft) long and weighing 3 tons. The males collect females to form harems. The walrus is a large pinniped, closely related to the sea lion, and has two long incisor teeth that form tusks. Sea lions move over dry land faster than seals, using all four limbs. Unlike the seals, they have external ears. Sea lions are numerous in the southern hemisphere, while only a few are found in the northern Pacific. During the breeding season, they congregate in huge colonies. Pinnipeds live in almost every ocean, but because they have been hunted for their fur and blubber, some species are endangered. For example, the

spotted dolphins (*Stenella frontalis*)

monk seal has almost totally disappeared from the Mediterranean Sea.

The cetaceans: whales and dolphins

The cetaceans are descended from prehistoric ungulates that returned to the sea. They now cannot live on land. So mating, birth, and care of young take place in water. The cetaceans include the largest animal that has ever lived, the blue whale. An adult can be 35 m (115 ft) long and weigh 150 tons. All cetaceans have a tapered body ending in a horizontal caudal (tail) fin, the fluke. Their hind legs have completely disappeared, and their forelegs have evolved into fins. The nostrils are on top of the head, an opening called the **blowhole**. Cetaceans can dive to depths of several hundred meters and hold their breath for more than an hour. Some species emit ultrasonic sounds that they use to communicate and to detect their prey. There are two main groups of cetaceans: the baleen whales and the toothed whales. The baleen whales include the humpback whale and the rorquals. Instead of teeth they have horny plates, or **baleens**, which they use to filter sea water to extract small fish and shrimp (krill). The toothed whales include the dolphins (including the killer whale), porpoises, beaked whales, and sperm whales. They have several dozen identical cone-shaped teeth and hunt fishes and squid. They are found in all the oceans, and some species live in fresh water. Dolphins, which comprise some forty species, live in schools and communicate using a language that scientists are attempting to decipher. Dolphins are social animals and come to the aid of a wounded or sick companion. The sperm whale can dive to a depth of 1,000 m (3,300 ft) to catch large squid. Digestive residues that accumulate in its intestines form ambergris, a substance used in the perfume industry. ☐

The killer whale

A voracious carnivore, the orca or killer whale, preys on seals, penguins, sea lions (above), and even whales. It sometimes runs aground when it comes too near the shore while pursuing prey.

A humpback whale (*Megaptera novaeangliae*) leaping clear of the water reveals its long fins covered with lumps.

ring-tailed lemur (*Lemur catta*) from Madagascar

The primates

The proboscis monkey

The proboscis monkey (*Nasalis larvatus*) lives in the damp forests on the coasts of the island of Borneo (Indonesia). It lives in the trees, where it finds its basic food, leaves. It is an excellent swimmer and swims underwater without hesitation. In the mornings and evenings, the trees and riverbanks resound with its echoing cries. This Old World monkey owes it name to its bizarre nose. The females and juveniles have pointed, long noses while the male's grows larger and droops in front of its mouth, as can be seen in the illustration above.

The woolly spider monkey (*Brachyteles arachnoides*) owes its name to its long arms and its thick coat.

The primates were so named by the Swedish naturalist Linnaeus in 1758. They were, in his words, the "first" in the classification of the animal kingdom. Fifty million years ago, the primates were all small nocturnal insectivores. The modern primates are divided into two

groups: the prosimians (such as the lemurs and tarsiers), and the simians, or monkeys, to which human beings and our ancestors belong. The primate brain is more developed than that of other mammals, and the structure of the skull is different. The eyes face forward, which gives good depth perception and helps to judge distances. Primates are plantigrades (they walk by placing the sole of the foot or hand flat on the ground). They can pick up objects, since the thumb can be opposed to the other digits.

Lemurs and tarsiers: prosimians

The prosimians are numerous in Madagascar and also live in Africa and Asia. They are arboreal (tree-dwelling), feeding mainly on leaves and fruit, and occasionally on insects and small birds. The strangest of the lemurs is undoubtedly the aye-aye. It has a very long finger that it uses to dislodge insects from beneath bark. The lesser mouse lemur is the smallest lemur, about the size of a rat. The tarsier looks like a small lemur, with a long tail, huge eyes, and highly evolved feet.

These gelada baboons (*Theropithecus gelada*) live in Africa.

Grooming is a ritual among chimpanzees (*Pan troglodytes*).

Tarsiers seem to be a link between the prosimians and the monkeys.

Marmosets, macaques, and baboons

Like the prosimians, monkeys are tree-dwellers and have an omnivorous diet (although they are mainly vegetarians). Two kinds are distinguished, the New World monkeys (from the Americas) and the Old World monkeys (from Africa and Asia). The New World monkeys, such as the small marmosets and spider monkeys, have from 32 to 36 teeth and widely separated nostrils. Using their long arms, they can swing from tree to tree. Their tail is usually prehensile, that is, it can grasp branches. The Old World monkeys (macaques, baboons, mandrills, proboscis monkeys) all have 32 teeth and close-set nostrils and do not have prehensile tails. Many species spend much of their time on the ground. In Africa, baboons live in groups called troops: the males have impressive canine teeth and will confront large predators such as leopards. When threatened, they take shelter in trees. Found across North Africa and numerous in Asia, macaques, such as the rhesus monkey, live in groups. It was in the rhesus monkey that the rhesus factor distinguishing human blood groups was first discovered.

a young orangutan (*Pongo pygmaeus*)

Gibbons, orangutans, gorillas, and chimpanzees

These apes lack tails and are thought to be the animals most closely related to humans, hence their name, anthropoids (from the Greek *anthropos*, "man"). The gibbons of southeast Asia are the smallest anthropoid apes. They almost never leave the trees, through which they swing using their long arms. The rare orangutan inhabits the forests of Sumatra and Borneo (Indonesia): it is a large, shy animal that normally keeps to the trees. Gorillas are the largest of the apes. Males can be up to 2 m (over 6 ft) tall and can weigh 250 kg (550 pounds). They live in groups in central and western Africa.

Chimpanzees are smaller and spend more time in trees, building a nest each evening to sleep in. Chimpanzees can make and use simple tools such as stick-probes, and their behavior seems to be closest to our own. Indeed, humans and chimpanzees have a common ancestor: the prehistoric ape *Ramapithecus.*   □

The mandrill

A close relative of the baboons, the mandrill (*Papio sphinx*) is a large Old World monkey that lives in the equatorial forest and wooded regions of West Africa. It spends much of its time on the ground but settles in trees to sleep. Mandrills live in family groups formed by a male, several females, and their young. The male, like the one pictured below, is more colorful than the female. The gaudy colors of its face are startling. Its brilliant red nose is emphasized on each side by wide bright blue ribbing. Its lips are also red, and its buttocks are red and blue. With impressively large canines, an angry mandrill is a formidable opponent.

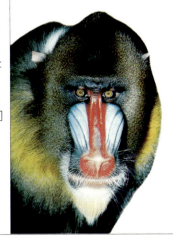

?

What is a naturalist?
A person who studies animals, minerals and plants.

What is a zoologist?
A person who studies animals.

What is a botanist?
A person who studies plants.

What is a biologist?
A person who studies living organisms, their growth and reproduction.

Did you know?

Which trees live the longest?
The bristlecone pines (*Pinus aristata*) that grow in the Sierra Nevada of California (United States). According to some estimates, they can live for 6,000 years. The oldest currently known, nicknamed "Methuselah," is 4,600 years old. Giant sequoia trees do not live so long (between 2,000 and 2,500 years), but are the largest of all trees: they can grow to a height of 110 m (360 ft).

How do animals in polar regions withstand the cold?
The polar bear has hollow hairs that conduct sunlight to its skin, which is black and absorbs the heat of the sun's rays. The bodies of insects inhabiting frozen regions produce a substance similar to the antifreeze used in car engines, and this prevents them from turning into icicles. These polar insects can withstand temperatures of –30°C (–22°F).

For how long does the marmot hibernate?
This mammal sleeps for 160 days. Its temperature drops from 37.5°C to 10°C (99.5°F to 50°F), and its heart rate slows from 88 to 15 beats a minute. Other animals live through long periods of inactivity: eelworms, a type of roundworm, can remain inactive in the ground

for up to 27 years, not because of cold, but because of drought. They are revived when they come into contact with water.

How do trees defend themselves against caterpillars?
When caterpillars attack the leaves of a tree, the tree begins to produce leaves that have a different chemical composition. Less nutritive and more difficult to digest, these gradually kill the caterpillars. It is even thought that a tree attacked by caterpillars can warn its fellow trees by emitting a gas that serves as an alarm signal.

Which mammal stays longest in its mother's womb?
The elephant calf remains in the uterus for between 21 and 22 months (a human baby is born after nine months). At the other extreme, the hamster gives birth after a gestation period of 16 days.

Where are the greatest number of insect species found?
In the Amazonian tropical forest in South America, or more precisely in its canopy (the upper level formed by the tree tops), where between 10 and 30 million species of insects have been recorded. This research was carried out using "a tree-top raft," a wooden

platform carried by a hot-air balloon and set down on top of the canopy.

How did dung beetles save the pastures of Australia?
The dung of innumerable cattle grazing on Australian pastures gradually covered huge areas and prevented the grass from resprouting. To remedy the situation, dung beetles were introduced: these small insects roll up animal excrement into pellets and bury it.

What is the longest distance traveled by a migratory butterfly?
Monarch butterflies travel nearly 3,000 km (1,900 miles) from Canada to Mexico, where they spend the winter before returning. They gather each year on the same trees in a region of Mexico that has been dubbed the "valley of the butterflies." The monarch is the only insect to make a two-way migration.

Famous people

Aristotle
(384–322 B.C.)
This great philosopher of ancient Greece was also one of the first to take a scientific interest in animals. In his books on living organisms, he described around 400 species, which he classified into vertebrates and invertebrates.

Pliny the Elder
(A.D. 23–79)
A Roman naturalist and writer who was the author of the first known major scientific encyclopaedia, *Natural History*, dedicated to the study of animals, plants, and rocks.

Comte de Buffon
(1707–1788)
A French naturalist and writer who was one of the pioneers of natural history. He wrote the 36-volume *Histoire Naturelle*, illustrated with many

drawings, in which he examined the behavior and way of life of each animal species.

Carl von Linné (Linnaeus)
(1707–1778)
The Swedish botanist who devised Latin double names for the animals and plants. The first Latin name corresponds to the genus and the second to the

species. This classification system is still used by biologists today.

Jean-Baptiste de Monet, Chevalier de Lamarck
(1744–1829)
A French zoologist who created a science derived from natural history, which he named biology. He proposed the first classification of invertebrates. He was also the author of the first theory of evolution, demonstrating that animals did not always retain the same characteristics and that they had evolved over the centuries.

Charles Darwin
(1809–1882)
An English naturalist who made a voyage around the world in the course of which he noticed that animals of the same family

may take a different form depending on where they live. On his return to England, he elaborated his theory of evolution of living organisms and of natural selection. His

book, *On the Origin of Species* (1859), made him famous.

Henry Walter Bates
(1825–1892)
An English naturalist, he discovered more than 8,000 hitherto unknown animal species in his explorations of the Amazon basin in South America. On his return, he published an essay on animal mimicry—that is, the capacity that some animals have for imitating another animal's shape, behavior, and color in order to escape predators. He was the first to give a scientific explanation for this.

Karl Von Frisch
(1886–1982)
An Austrian biologist who is today known as "the professor of the bees," for he was the first

to decode their language. He noticed that when a bee has found food, it tells other bees how to find it by performing a sort of dance.

Konrad Lorenz
(1903–1989)
An Austrian zoologist famous for his investigations into animal behavior. He noticed that some young animals attach themselves to the first living being they encounter just after birth. He called this phenomenon "imprinting."

Jane Goodall
(born 1934)
An English naturalist who went to study chimpanzees in Gombe National Park, Tanzania, Africa. After two years of patient tracking, she was able to approach the animals and made valuable discoveries about their social behavior. She established the Jane Goodall Institute for the conservation of chimpanzees.

Index

Crédits photographiques

Couverture : *Champs de tournesols (Helianthus annuus)* : Bavaria/Bildagentur – Pix ; *Femelle guépard et son petit (Acinonyx jubatus)* : De Wilde P. – Hoa-Qui ; *Kelp (macrocystis pyrifera)* : De Wilde S. ; *Punaises rouges (pyrrhocoris apterus)* : Lopez G. - Bios ; *Rainettes d'Amérique du Sud (Agalychnis callidryas)* : Odum A. – Bios
Dos de couverture : *Papillon flambeau (Bryas julia)* : Wiewandt T. – Pix
Pages de garde : *Détail d'une aile de papillon machaon (Papilio machaon)* : Lorne P. – Jacana
Page titre : *Rainettes du Costa Rica (Agalychnis callidryas)* : Odum A. – Bios

p. 2-h *Jeune orang-outan (Pongo pygmaeus)* : Ruoso C. – Bios
p. 2-b *Eponge tubulaire (Verognia lacunosa)* : Bavendam F. – Bios
p. 3-m1 Lorne P.
p. 3-m2 Lorne P.
p. 3-m3 Lorne P.
p. 3-m4 Lorne P.
p. 3-m5 Lorne P.
p. 3-m6 Lorne P.
p. 4-hg Ferrero-Labat – Jacana
p. 4-mh Viard M. – Jacana
p. 4-hd Gladu Y. – Jacana
p. 4-mhg De Wilde S.
p. 4-mg Cavignaux R. – Bios
p. 4-mbg Monel Y. – Map
p. 4-md De Wilde S.
p. 4-mbd Goetgheluck P.
p. 4-b *Elephants (Loxodonta africana)* : Laboureur M. – Bios
p. 5-hg Lorne P. – Jacana
p. 5-mh Polking – Jacana
p. 5-hd Denis-Huot M. –Bios
p. 5-mhg De Wilde S.
p. 5-mg Carmichael J. – NHPA
p. 5-mbg Panda Photo/Gaslini G. – Bios
p. 5-mhd Gohier F. – Jacana
p. 5-md Wildlife/Harvey – Bios
p. 5-mbd Gunther M. – Bios
p. 5-b *Toucan (Ramphastus sulfuratus)* : Planet Earth/Farneti C. – Pix
p. 6-hg *Bourdon (Bombus) butinant une fleur de pissenlit* : Bringard D. – Bios
p. 6-h *Amanites tue-mouche (Amanita muscaria)* : Delobelle J.P. – Bios
p. 6-mh *Fougères* : Ferrero-Labat – Jacana
p. 6-mb *Nénuphars (Nymphea)* : Cavignaux R. – Bios
p. 6-b *Bogues de chataîgnes (Castanea sativa)* : Monel Y. – Map
p. 7-h *Orme de Sibérie bonsaï (Ulmus parviflolia)* : Goetgheluck P.
p. 7-b *Branche de mélèze d'Europe (Larix decidua)* : Klein-Hubert – Bios
p. 8-hg *Sous-bois d'une forêt tropicale* : Pix
p. 8-h1 De Wilde S.
p. 8-h2 Thouvenin G. – Jacana
p. 8-h3 Gladu Y.
p. 8-m1 Secchi-Lecaque/Roussel-Uclaf – C.N.R.I.
p. 8-m2 C.N.R.I.
p. 8-b1 Grospas J.-Y. – Bios
p. 9-h Desmier X. – VISA
p. 9-h1 Rodriguez – Jacana
p. 9-h2 Le Toquin A. – Jacana
p. 9-h3 Grospas J.-Y. – Bios
p. 9-h4 Klein-Hubert – Bios
p. 9-h5 Bertrand – Bios
p. 9-b1 Delobelle J.-P. – Bios
p. 10-h *Morilles coniques (Morchella conica deliciosa)* : Lanceau Y.
p. 10-b Lanceau Y.
p. 11-h Delobelle J.-P. – Bios
p. 11-m Lanceau Y.
p. 11-b Grospas J.-Y. – Bios
p. 12-hg *Algue verte (Enteromorpha linga)* : Le Toquin A.
p. 12-m Le Toquin A.
p. 12-b De Wilde S.
p. 13-h De Wilde S.
p. 13-hd Carré C. – Jacana
p. 13-bd SPL/Kage M. – Cosmos
p. 13-b Nardin C. – Jacana
p. 14-h Le Toquin A. – Jacana
p. 14-b Planet Earth/Maitland D. – Pix
p. 15-h Grospas J.-Y. – Bios
p. 15-mg Grospas J.-Y. – Bios
p. 15-bg Starosta P.
p. 15-md Compost A. – Bios
p. 15-bd Starosta P.
p. 16-h Le Moigne J.-L. – Jacana
p. 16-g Klein-Hubert – Bios
p. 16/17 Somelet P. – Diaf
p. 17-h Klein-Hubert – Bios
p. 17-mg Klein-Hubert – Bios
p. 17-md Brun J. – Jacana
p. 17-bd Mioulane N.et P. – Map
p. 18-h *Rafflesia d'Indonésie (Rafflesia)* : Visage-Compost – PHO.N.E.
p. 18-m Dulhoste R. – Jacana
p. 19-h Cavignaux R. – Bios
p. 19-md Planet Earth/Eastcott & Momatiuk – Pix
p. 19-bg Bringard D. – Bios
p. 19-bd Larivière A. – Jacana
p. 20/21 Goetgheluck P.
p. 21-hd *Protea (Protea)* : Denis-Huot M. – Bios
p. 22-h Pambour B. – Bios
p. 22-hg Gunther M. – Bios
p. 22-bg Brun J. – Jacana
p. 22-b Berthoule H. – Jacana
p. 23-h Masterfile – Pix
p. 23-m Layer W. – Jacana
p. 23-bd Viard M. – Jacana
p. 23-b Frebet J. – Bios
p. 24-h Dalton S. – NHPA
p. 24-b Burton J. – Bruce Coleman
p. 25-h Planet Earth/Eastcott & Momatiuk – Pix
p. 25-hd Monel Y. – Map
p. 25-m Grospas J.-Y. – Bios
p. 25-bg Lecourt D. – Jacana
p. 25-bd Grospas J.-Y. – Bios
p. 26-h Klein-Hubert – Bios
p. 26-g Starosta P.
p. 26-b Lacoste L. – Jacana
p. 27-h Douillet J. – Bios
p. 27-m Fotogram-Stone
p. 27-hd Thomas J.P. – Jacana
p. 27-b Pilloud P. – Jacana
p. 27-bd Kiefer H. – Figaro Madame
p. 28-h Viard M. – Jacana
p. 28-mg König R. – Jacana
p. 28-bg Viard M. – Jacana
p. 28-bd Thomas J.-P. – Jacana
p. 29-h Olivon P. – Jacana
p. 29-hd Delobelle J.-P. – Bios
p. 29-bg Nuridsany et Pérennou
p. 29-bd Volot R. – Jacana
p. 30-hg *Tête de ténia (Taenia saginata)* : C.N.R.I.
p. 30-h *Gorgone jaune de Méditérannée (Eucinella cavolini)* : De Wilde S. – Jacana
p. 30-mh *Escargots de jardin (Cepaea)* : Roche J. – Bios
p. 30-mb *Punaise gendarme (Pyrrhocoris apterus)* : Lopez G. – Bios
p. 30-b *Homard (Homarus vulgaris)* : De Wilde S.
p. 31-h *Etoile de mer biscuit (Tosia)* : De Wilde S.
p. 31-b *Papillon comète en ponte (Argema mittrei)* : Heuclin D. – Bios
p. 32-hg *Mille-pattes enroulé* : Bernard G.I. – NHPA
p. 32-h1 Secchi-Lecaque/Roussel-Uclaf – C.N.R.I.
p. 32-h2 C.N.R.I.
p. 32-m1 Gladu Y. – Jacana
p. 32-h3 De Wilde S. – Jacana
p. 33-h De Wilde S.
p. 33-h1 C.N.R.I.
p. 33-h2 Révy J.-C. – C.N.R.I.
p. 33-h3 Prévost J. – Bios
p. 33-h4 De Wilde S.
p. 33-h5 De Wilde S. – Jacana
p. 33-b1 Ziegler J.-L. – Bios
p. 33-b2 Goetgheluck P.
p. 33-b3 Bain J. – NHPA
p. 33-b4 S.P.L./Read M. – Cosmos
p. 33-bd Serrette D./Paléontologie – Muséum national d'Histoire naturelle, Paris
p. 34-h *Eponge brune des Bahamas (Agelus conifera)* : De Wilde S.
p. 34-b Bavendam F. – Bios
p. 35-h Gladu Y. – Jacana
p. 35-mg Planet Earth/Atkinson P. – Pix
p. 35-m Lanceau Y. – Jacana
p. 35-md Parks P. – NHPA
p. 35-b Bavendam F. – Bios
p. 36-h *Sangsue médicinale (Hirudo medicinalis)* : Chaumeton H. – Jacana
p. 36-b Bavendam F. – Bios
p. 37-h De Wilde S.
p. 37-md Révy J.C. – C.N.R.I.
p. 37-mg Ferrero J.-P. – Jacana
p. 37-b C.N.R.I.
p. 38-hg *Limace rouge (Arion rufus)* : Dulhoste R. – Jacana
p. 38-b Génétiaux N.
p. 39-m Labat-Lanceau – Jacana
p. 39-h Roche J. – Bios
p. 39-hd Soury G. – Jacana
p. 39-bd Laboute P. – Jacana
p. 40-h *Lycose portant oeufs sur son dos (Lycosa)* : Heuclin D. – Bios
p. 40-m Bringard D. – Bios
p. 40/41 Planet Earth/Gasson P. – Pix
p. 41-h Lorne P. – Jacana
p. 41-mg Heuclin D. – Bios
p. 41-md Bringard D. – Bios
p. 41-b Lorne P. – Jacana
p. 42-h De Wilde S.
p. 42-mg Parks P. – NHPA
p. 42-md König R. – Jacana
p. 42-b Carré C. – Jacana
p. 43-h De Wilde S.
p. 43-m Winner F. – Jacana
p. 43-b König R. – Jacana
p. 44-h Thonnerieux Y. – Bios
p. 44-mg Lopez G. – Bios
p. 44-b Heuclin D. – Bios
p. 44-md Bringard D. – Bios
p. 45-h SPL/Read M. – Cosmos
p. 45-m Etienne J.-J. – Bios
p. 45-b Rouxaime – Jacana
p. 46-h Cavignaux R. – Bios
p. 46-b Guihard C. – Bios
p. 46-mg Varin J.-P. – Jacana
p. 47-h Lopez G. – Bios
p. 47-g Dalton S. – NHPA
p. 47-md SPL/Wadforth C. – Cosmos
p. 47-bd Bassot J.-M. – Jacana
p. 48/49 Goetgheluck P.
p. 49-hd *Coccinelles (Coccinella septempunctata)* : Rebouleau B. – Jacana
p. 50-h Etienne J.-J. – Bios
p. 50-hg Bannister A. – NHPA
p. 50-bg Goetgheluck P.
p. 50-d Goetgheluck P.
p. 51-h Goetgheluck P.
p. 51-m1 Lorne P.
p. 51-m2 Lorne P.
p. 51-m3 Lorne P.
p. 51-m4 Lorne P.
p. 51-m5 Lorne P.
p. 51-b Goetgheluck P.
p. 52-h *Etoile de mer d'Australie (Echinodermata asteroidea)* : De Wilde S. – Jacana
p. 52-m Rotman J. – Bios
p. 53-h De Wilde S. – Jacana
p. 53-m Chaumeton H. – Jacana
p. 53-bd Danrigal F. – Jacana
p. 53-b De Wilde S.
p. 54-hg *Grenouille (Hyla arborea)* : Dalton S. – NHPA
p. 54-h *Paon faisant la roue (Pavo cristatus)* : Ferrero J.-P. – Jacana
p. 54-mh *Girelle paon (Thalossoma pavo)* : De Wilde S.
p. 54-mb *Eléphants (Loxodonta africana)* : Ferrero-Labat – Jacana
p. 54-b *Renards roux, femelle et son petit (Vulpes vulpes)* : Danegger M. – Jacana
p. 55-h *Gibbon à mains blanches (Hylobates lar)* : Brun J. – Jacana
p. 55-b *Caméléon panthère (Chamaeleofurcifer pardalis)* : Dani C. – Jeske I. – Bios
p. 56-hg *Iguane marin des Galapagos (Amblyrhynchus cristatus)* : McDonald T. – NHPA
p. 56-h1 Snyderman M. – Planet Earth Pictures
p. 56-h2 Taylor R. & V. – Ardea
p. 56-h3 Schauer J. – Fricke H.
p. 56-m1 Soury G. – Jacana
p. 57-h Denis-Huot M. – Bios
p. 57-h1 Lefevre Y. – Bios
p. 57-h2 Compost A. – Bios
p. 57-h3 Labat J.-M. – Jacana
p. 57-h4 Ferrero-Labat – Jacana
p. 57-m1 Wild P. – Jacana
p. 57-m2 Heuclin D. – Bios
p. 57-m3 Dennis N. – NHPA
p. 57-m4 Seitre R. – Bios
p. 57-bd Serrette D./PalÇontologie – Muséum national d'Histoire naturelle, Paris
p. 58-h *Brochet (Esox lucius)* : Noë – Lutra
p. 58-b Ribette M. – Bios
p. 58/59 Marielle B. – Bios
p. 59-h De Wilde S.
p. 59-hd Schauer J. – Fricke H.
p. 59-b Heuclin D. – Bios
p. 60-h Rotman J. – Bios
p. 60-hg De Wilde S.
p. 60-m Garguil P. – Bios
p. 60-hd Marielle B. – Bios
p. 60-b Soury G. – Jacana
p. 60-bg Gladu Y. – Jacana
p. 61-h Sylvestre J.-P. – Bios
p. 61-hd De Wilde S. – Jacana
p. 61-b Lutra
p. 62-h Rotman J. – Bios
p. 62-hg Planet Earth/Bell G. – Pix
p. 62-b Panda Photo/Watt J. – Bios
p. 62/63 Panda Photo/Watt J. – Bios
p. 63-h Labat-Lanceau – Jacana
p. 63-hd Quillivic C.G. – Bios
p. 63-b Soury G. – Jacana
p. 64-h *Salamandre tachetée (Salamandra salamandra)* : Milos A. – Bios
p. 64-m Davenne J.-M. – Jacana
p. 65-h Odum A. – Bios
p. 65-m Bringard D. – Bios
p. 65-hd Dalton S. – NHPA
p. 65-mh Dalton S. – NHPA
p. 65-mb Bernard G.-I. – NHPA
p. 65-bd Heuclin D. – Bios
p. 65-bg PHR/HIGFILL KM – Jacana
p. 66-h *Tortue de mer (Chelonia mydas)* : Planet Earth/Perrine D. – Pix
p. 66-b Gohier F. – Jacana
p. 67-h, Seitre R. – Bios
p. 67-hd Grospas J.-Y. – Bios
p. 67-hg Brun J. – Jacana
p. 67-md Heuclin D. – Bios
p. 67-b König R. – Jacana
p. 68-h Loup M. – Jacana
p. 68-m Poulard J. – Jacana
p. 68-b Heuclin D. – Bios
p. 69-h Carmichael J. – NHPA
p. 69-hg Carmichael J. – NHPA
p. 69-hd Moiton C.et M. – Jacana
p. 69-bd Rouxaime – Jacana
p. 69-b Heuclin D. – Bios
p. 70/71 Dalton S. – NHPA
p. 71-hd *Grande sauterelle verte (Tettigonia viridissima)* : Lorne P. – Jacana
p. 72-h *Oeufs de grive musicienne (Turdus philomenos)* : Martin G. – Bios
p. 72/73 Axel – Jacana
p. 72-b Wisniewski W. – Jacana
p. 73-h Panda Photo/Gaslini G. – Bios
p. 73-b Eichaker X. – Bios
p. 74-h Ferrero J.-P. – Jacana
p. 74-hg Lundberg B. – Bios
p. 74-bd Halleux D. – Bios
p. 74-bg Bannister A. – NHPA
p. 75-h Dalton S. – NHPA
p. 75-m Dalton S. – NHPA
p. 75-bg Seitre R. – Bios
p. 75-bd Pons A. – Bios
p. 76-h Cordier S. – Jacana
p. 76-hg Halleux D. – Bios
p. 76-b Thomas T. – Bios
p. 77-h Seitre R. – Bios
p. 77-m Hellio J.-F.-Van Ingen N. – Jacana
p. 77-bd Hellio J.-F.-Van Ingen N. – Jacana
p. 77-bg Frédéric – Jacana
p. 78-h Seitre R. – Bios
p. 78-hg Hellio J.-F.-Van Ingen N. – Jacana
p. 78-m Lundberg B. – Bios
p. 78-b Alcalay J. – Bios
p. 79-h ADN – Bios
p. 79-m Layer W. – Jacana
p. 79-b Grey M. – NHPA
p. 80-h Delfino D. – Bios
p. 80-bg Dennis N. – NHPA
p. 80-hg Beehler B. – NHPA
p. 80-hd Varin-Visage – Jacana
p. 81-h Saunier A. – Jacana
p. 81-hd Nigel D. – Jacana
p. 81-b Layer W. – Jacana
p. 82-hg *Echidné de Bruijn (Zaglossus bruij)* : Cordier S. – Jacana
p. 82-hd Palo H. – NHPA
p. 82-b Ziesler G. – Jacana
p. 83-h Auscape/Parer-Cook – Jacana
p. 83-m Klein-Hubert – Bios
p. 83-b Klein-Hubert – Bios
p. 84-h Danneger M. – Jacana
p. 84-m Sauvanet J. – Bios
p. 84-hg Dalton S. – NHPA
p. 84-bg Gohier F. – PHO.N.E.
p. 85-h Gohier F. – Jacana
p. 85-m Dalton S. – NHPA
p. 85-hd Dalton S. – NHPA
p. 86-h Danegger M. – Jacana
p. 86-hg Klein-Hubert – Bios
p. 86-b Soder E. – Jacana
p. 87-h Dalton S. – NHPA
p. 87-hg Pierrel F. – Bios
p. 87-hd Klein-Hubert – Bios
p. 87-b Bannister A. – NHPA
p. 88-h Wisniewski W. – Jacana
p. 88-hg Amsler K. – Jacana
p. 88-b Cavignaux R. – Bios
p. 88/89 Denis-Huot M. – Bios
p. 89-h Denis-Huot M. – Bios
p. 89-m Layer W. – Jacana
p. 89-b Sourd C. – Bios
p. 90-h Cordier S. – Jacana
p. 90-hd Held S.
p. 90-bg Denis-Huot M. – Bios
p. 90-bd Walker T. – Jacana
p. 91-h Shah A. – Jacana
p. 91-hd Varin J.-P. – Jacana
p. 91-b Ferrero-Labat – Jacana
p. 92/93 Degré A. – Jacana
p. 93-hd *Désert du Kalahari* : Gunther M. – Bios
p. 94-h Wildlife/Harvey – Bios
p. 94-hg Danegger M. – Jacana
p. 94-hd Tietz T. – Fotogram-Stone
p. 94-b Ferrero-Labat – PHO.N.E.
p. 95-h Pierrel F. – Bios
p. 95-hd Pu Tao – Bios
p. 95-b Ferrero-Labat – Jacana
p. 96-h Bruemmer F. – Bios
p. 96-hd Visage A. – PHO.N.E.
p. 96-b Ausloos H. – Bios
p. 97-h Gohier F. – Jacana
p. 97-hd Auscape/Parer D. & Parer-Cook E. – PHO.N.E.
p. 97-b Gohier F. – Jacana
p. 98-h Loup M. – Jacana
p. 98-hg Ruoso C. – Bios
p. 98-hd Seitre R. – Bios
p. 98-b Gunther M. – Bios
p. 99-h Gunther M. – Bios
p. 99-m Ruoso C. – Bios
p. 99-b Lanceau Y. – Jacana
p. 100-hg Biblio. centrale – Muséum national d'Histoire naturelle, Paris
p. 100-bg Biblio. centrale – Muséum national d'Histoire naturelle, Paris
p. 101-mh Biblio. centrale – Muséum national d'Histoire naturelle, Paris
p. 101-hd Biblio. centrale – Muséum national d'Histoire naturelle, Paris
p. 101-hg Biblio. centrale – Muséum national d'Histoire naturelle, Paris
p. 101-mhg Biblio. centrale – Muséum national d'Histoire naturelle, Paris
p. 101-mhd Biblio. centrale – Muséum national d'Histoire naturelle, Paris
p. 101-hd Biblio. centrale – Muséum national d'Histoire naturelle, Paris
p. 101-bg Coll. Larousse
p. 101-mg National Museum, Stockholm
p. 101-md National Gallery, Londres
p. 101-d Gamma
p. 101-bd Zalewski S. – Bios

Illustrateur

Jean-Claude Senée : p. 9, 11, 19, 23, 29.

Photogravure : Arrigo, Bordeaux - Mame Imprimeurs, Tours - Dépôt légal septembre 1995 - N° de série éditeur : 18983
Imprimé en France (Printed in France) 652424 A, juin 2000